59,50

In Search of New

Maarten Hajer
Arnold Reijndorp

Public Domain

Analysis and Strategy

NAi Publishers

The Public Domain as Perspective

Introduction

The Ramblas in Barcelona, the Corbières in Marseille and Lake Shore Drive in Chicago are locations that have practically become clichéd references for generations of designers, architects and urban planners. They are presented as the highest ideal for new public spaces. They are examples of spaces that have a strong public significance; places with which people identify and make the city what it is, an integral part of urban identity. However, at the same time it remains unclear what exactly defines the strengths of these examples. It is true that we recognize the quality of these and other celebrated examples of public spaces, but we are unable to specify the success factors.

What are the characteristics of 'good' public space? To what extent can good public space be artificially created? These are questions that are central to this essay. More especially, for us the question revolves around what the design disciplines (architecture, urbanism and landscape architecture) can contribute to the creation of these public places in the city. Following on from this we want to establish what strategic framework this generates for policy.

Since the late 1980s, the public space has been a subject of intense interest. It is the key to urban renewal strategies all over the world. The approach to parks and squares in Barcelona and Paris forms the inspiration for designers and administrators, the development of 'waterfronts' in the cities on the east coast of North America has been imitated everywhere, and since the 1990s the New Urbanism has swiftly won support.

The re-evaluation of the urban public space in a city such as Birmingham, England, can serve as a model for the situation in countless cities, in Europe and beyond. Under the direction of noted British planner Sir

Herbert Manzoni, a system of 'ring roads' and 'relief roads' was developed here in the 1960s. The city centre had to be made accessible, but in fact it was cut off: the public space came to be dominated by motorized traffic. In the meantime perceptions have changed. The car is being forced out, squares and streets have been newly designed, and citizens have rediscovered the public space as a space to spend their time. The squares that were cut into pieces have been restored to their former glory, parking spaces have been shifted to improve sight lines, and new public spaces are being created. The citizens who had learnt to avoid the city are starting to visit it again.

Deceptive consensus

The broad reassessment of the meaning of the public space is treacherous territory. Why do we think the public space in Birmingham functions better now than previously? Because it looks more pretty? Because there are more people walking around? Because it is safer on the street? Because there is more investment, or more spending? Because tourism has grown? Because it has improved Birmingham's image?

The public space is unequivocally important for new urban planning strategies. We also tend to think that the public space fulfils an important role in increasing the 'social cohesion' in society. But the explanation of the exact significance of the public space remains an implicit one. What are the factors that actually constitute this elusive quality?

One of the reasons for the lack of a vision as regards the quality of the public space lies in the fact that important 'players' such as administrators, designers and developers to a large degree think along the same lines, at least at the moment, when it comes to the design of that urban public space. There are a number of clearly defined 'design discourses' that determine the reorganization of urban spaces everywhere. The similarities between the retro-romantic reconstruction projects in Berlin, The Hague and Birmingham are just as eye-catching as those between late-modern projects in Barcelona, Rotterdam and Paris. Common themes include the interest in the reduction of untidiness, an emphasis on the aesthetic, and a predilection for design.

We gain a different perspective when we focus our gaze on the state of the public space in general, rather than taking the trendsetting designs as the starting point. The celebrated and often photographed new aesthetics of the public spaces of Barcelona, Birmingham, Rotterdam or Berlin are only occasionally mentioned in the same breath as the problems encountered in other public spaces in those same cities. At the same time, there is still an approach to the public space that focuses on themes such as lack of safety and 'mindless' violence. This also generates new ideas for the organization or reorganization of the public space. The control of the fear for violence has become a weighty theme in the expansion and the rearrangement of the city (Davis 1998). This gives a completely new meaning to the concept of 'defensible urban space', once introduced to denote the value of the small-scale in the big city (Newman 1972; see also Jacobs 1961). The design of the public space becomes an aspect of its manageability. In a growing number of cities, the safety discussion leads to the introduction of omnipresent closed-circuit surveillance cameras. In other cities, the mobilization of private security services has become a point of discussion. In formal terms this does by definition not negate the public character of the space. However, with solutions that go just a step further, this can indeed be the case. The most simple solution for dangerous squares and parks is to simply phase them out by building on them or privatizing them. A comparable strategy is the demolition of so-called problem complexes. Over the coming years, the call for simple solutions to complex social problems will also partly determine the way that the public space is rearranged.

A third perspective in today's debate about the public space is shaped by the broadly shared aversion for what the French anthropologist Marc Augé called 'non-places' (Augé 1992). Augé takes the emergence of perfunctorily functional transit spaces such as motorways, roadside restaurants, TGV stations and shopping malls as the crux of his thesis, and posits these in contrast to the 'anthropological' places that are socially and historically anchored. Compared with the qualities of the 19th-century station with its places for reposing, such as waiting rooms and restaurants, the modern airport is anonymous, focused on the handling of massive streams of 'passengers' rather than the traveller as individual. It is notable how Augé's thesis resonates among sociologists, philosophers and cultural critics, while many architects and architecture critics consider the phenomenon of the 'non-place' as an expression of the super-modern condition: it is marked by loneliness and constant change (Ibelings 1998). The first group struggles with unease about how this kind of semi-public space functions, while the second group is much more likely to see this development as inevitable. Whatever the case, the relationship between design and public space is at issue here too.

In short, there are at least three different ways in which we talk about the organization of the public space. Each of these lines of approach effectively forms a separate 'discourse', with its own standard solutions, sympathizers and blind spots. They basically form their own separate little worlds. It is therefore even more striking that solutions posited from these different viewpoints converge in an apparent consensus about the importance of the public space as a space for encounters, as well as with respect to its arrangement and management, under the motto: 'Beautiful, wholesome, and safe.' The distaste for Augé's 'non-places' vies with the call for safety that leads in effect to the privatization and control of urban public space. The emphasis on the function as meeting place is at odds with the exclusion, implicit or explicit, of certain groups who are considered marginal. In the course of time, the aesthetic ideal of designers and administrators is often negated by the concessions to the demands of users for pleasantness and more greenery.

The recognition of the importance of public space provides in itself few clues for determining what constitutes a 'good' public space. There is much less insight into the degree to which this can be deliberately created. What is the role of design in the development of good public space? What is the relationship between the design discourse and the diversity of requirements to which the public space is subject?

In our opinion, the answer to this question lies in the analysis of the objectives, often implicit, of cultural policy with regards to the public space. What do administrators, designers or users mean when they talk about the 'quality' of the public space? Views about the public and the urban underpin this, but what is meant by the encounter function of the public space? How are ideas about social cohesion and fear for segregation connected with this? What role do conflicting aesthetic ideas about authenticity, authorship, historic continuity, social relevance and avant-gardism play in the design process?

This essay aims to help in the crystallization of a cultural policy for the design of the public space. We are interested in the factors that lead certain places to develop into 'public domain'. We are interested in this from a specific viewpoint about the social and political importance of such a domain. We define 'public domain' as those places where an exchange between different social groups is possible and also actually occurs. Public domain is thereby a guiding ideal for us: it is a perspective from which we want to analyze the existing public space, because no matter how often lip service is paid to the objectives and desirability of a public domain, places only rarely seem to actually function in this way.

This highlights an analytical viewpoint that is a central and distinguishing feature of this book: the distinction between 'public space' and 'public domain'. Public space is in essence a space that is freely accessible for everyone: public is the opposite of private. That is not to say that every public space is a public domain. Public domain entails additional requirements. We are interested in the question of which spaces are positively valued as places of shared experience by people from different backgrounds or with dissimilar interests. In principle, such places can also be found beyond the traditional urban space of streets, parks and squares. They can even be spaces that are not public in the strict sense, for example privately managed collective spaces that still function as public domain. What in fact gives such places their public quality? To return to the example given above: the Ramblas is without question a public domain, but what gives it this quality? Why does this place have a central function in the city, both for its residents and for its visitors? Is it the specific location, is it the activities that take place there, or its function in the collective subconscious of the city? What role does the spatial design play? How can policy take advantage of this? These are the kinds of questions we will tackle here.

Public domain as urban space

In choosing the public domain as a context we are positioning ourselves in a lively and complex debate. After all, the term public domain is not only used to refer to the physical places in the city, but also has a broader political and philosophical meaning. Philosophers such as Hannah Arendt and Jürgen Habermas have often written about the 'public sphere' in society, and others also employ the term 'public domain' in a broader context.

In philosophical discussions the public sphere is the place where society is formed, or at least the arena where the collective will is formed with regards to the future of society. The public sphere then also denotes the whole apparatus of social institutions that fulfil a function within that sphere: newspapers, television, parliament, discussion forums. But the public realm, as it is also called, also occupies a unique place in society: it is the sphere where we encounter the proverbial 'other' and where we must relate to 'other' behaviour, other ideas and other preferences. This means it is also a domain of surprise and reflection. The public realm is 'the sphere of social relations going beyond our own circle of friend-ships, and of family and professional relations. The idea of the public realm is bound up with the ideas of expanding one's mental horizons, of experiment, adventure, discovery, surprise' (Bianchini & Schwengel 1991, p. 229).

The relation between the public sphere and the physical space is im-portant in our search for the conditions for the development of places into public domains. This relationship has been defined by various authors. Richard Sennett and Jürgen Habermas regard public places, such as the coffee houses of ages past, as institutions of middle-class society that play an important role in processes of social change. More recent literature by Sharon Zukin (1995), Rob Shields (1991) and Kevin Hetherington (1997) also underscores the importance of locations where physical meetings occur for the public sphere. The nature of that 'meeting' remains unclear, as do the requirements that the physical space must satisfy.

In our definition of public domain we have expressly elected to use the term 'exchange' rather than 'meeting'. We uphold this in concordance with the view of Immanuel Kant that making judgements is always based on an exchange with others. It is in this confrontation with other opinions that we develop our own ideas. 'Judging' is not simply the application of received norms. It is something that is based on becoming aware of one's own values and the decision to uphold these, or indeed to adapt them. We also assume that the concrete, physical experience of the presence of others, of other cultural manifestations, and of the confrontation with different meanings associated with the same physical space, is important for developing social intelligence and forming a judgement. Personal perception and direct confrontation can be an antidote to stereotyping and stigmatization. The term 'exchange' implies that such confrontations can also be symbolic. Popular metaphors such as 'the city as theatre' refer to the urban space as symbolic space, as a space where a battle of meanings is fought out. Our research into the conditions for the development of public domain does not stem from a moral calling, some kind of political correctness, but primarily stems from curiosity and a propensity for voyeurism, traits that we believe we share with other urbanites.

In this essay we emphatically restrict ourselves to the analysis of the physical places in urban society that function as public domain. We are seeking opportunities for creating spaces that facilitate 'cultural mobility': places where people can have new experiences, where a change of perspective is possible (see also Hajer & Halsema 1997).

We will not peremptorily restrict ourselves concerning the question of where we can find these places. Our impression is that the discussion about public space is too one-sidedly focused on the traditional urban space. In recent decades, urban society has changed radically; not just socially but also in a spatial sense. Social and spatial entities no longer inevitably coincide. The contradistinction between the city and its surrounding areas, between centre and periphery, has a different meaning and has in part become irrelevant. Our cultural-political quest requires a cultural geography in which it is not the functional relations that are central, but the cultural significance of places.

New tasks

The approach to the public domain outlined here comes at a moment when the public space is once again faced with a large-scale design task. Over the coming five years, stations for high-speed passenger train (HST) stations throughout Europe will be designed as new urban interchanges. Each of these can become a new public domain. But what notion of public space actually stands as the foundation for the design of these stations and their environs? What is the cultural programme of requirements that forms the basis for this design task? In addition, will inner cities have to safeguard their economic and socio-cultural future in the coming years? But how successful will the various strategies that are currently being drafted prove to be: the city as 'mall', the city as theme park, the city as historic residential enclave? And what are the consequences for urban society and the public domain? A third challenge is the concern about public violence. There is a growing sense of insecurity and government is under a great deal of pressure to take 'tough measures'. What kinds of spaces will be created by these new measures? What new divisions will they erect in the urban space and urban society?

It is only possible to answer these questions as if they are placed in the context of the new social and spatial patterns of the late-modern urban society. Given the enormous demand for single-family dwellings and mobility that is increasing at a rate faster than the growth in economic prosperity, is it reasonable to assume that the city will become increasingly disparate, in spatial and social terms, over the coming years. The rapid developments in the fields of information technology and telecommunications are an important factor, which mean that people are no longer tied to specific workplaces and that contacts in leisure time are organized in a completely different way. Due to people being reachable all the time by mobile phone, the notion of 'meeting place' has taken on a fundamentally different meaning. This expanded and mobile city implies a new agenda for the design of the public space, not only in the urban centres or in the new residential districts, but especially in the ambiguous in-between areas. What meaning do these places have for urban society, and how could that meaning best be reinforced? For example, though not necessarily public, can the new 'collective' spaces such as amusement parks, factory outlets and chain stores develop into new public domains?

If one takes the time to consider these design tasks, one realizes that the way in which we have thought about public space thus far has its shortcomings. We actually have no standard by which to ascertain the quality of public space. Moreover, a great deal of potential public domain is simply ignored. Politicians and other policy-makers seem as yet unconvinced that these will be the most important strategic questions for the coming years.

A good deal of the discussion about the public space is conducted in terms of decline and loss. In our opinion this pessimism is unsatisfactory as well as misplaced. The belief that we are marching towards an impasse in our attempts to create a 'better' public space seems to be the result of the framework that we employ for the public space. Sometimes we approach a problem with the wrong concepts and we are therefore unable to solve certain problems. Take, for example, the idea that public domain has been understood in terms of the 'bourgeois' public places of the Paris of the 18th century or Vienna at the end of the 19th century. What is the effect of using these reference points? Might we not be focusing too closely on those examples, instead of looking at the ways in which processes of exchange and mutual interest arise, and how they can be facilitated right now?

Sometimes it is as if we are simply incapable of recognizing certain qualities. A new conceptual language with which we can articulate opportunities and threats, problems and solutions in a new way may provide us with a new approach to the public domain.

The language that we use to talk about reality influences the way we comprehend that reality. The concept of 'discourse' or 'representation' indicates that there is often an implicit framework in our discussions about a certain theme. A discourse is thus described as a more or less coherent set of ideas and concepts used to define the meaning of specific empirical phenomena (Hajer 1995). Discourses often work as implicit mental frameworks in a discussion. As an expressly implicit frame, it is perfectly possible that those involved in a particular discourse do not initially recognize this themselves. If we wish to escape the prevailing approach to the public space, then an analysis of the influence of discourse is important. Following on from the ideas of Foucault, the discussion about public space will also be controlled by certain – implicit – intellectual frameworks or discourses. In other words, we do not think freely about public space, but according to specific 'discursive rules', which also structure our communication with others.

We will attempt to reconstruct a number of these rules here. The thinking about public space is, for example, all too often very clearly dominated by the dichotomy of city and periphery. This may mislead us. In our view, the thinking is also insufficiently inspired by the way in which 'meaning' emerges in the space. Why do people value some places and not others?

Furthermore, we seem to think too much about public space in the sense of fixed and permanent physical spaces, and we give insufficient consideration to the way in which public domain comes into being in places in flux, often extremely temporarily. The last question is to what extent the public space suffers under the all too oft-repeated ideal of the urban 'meeting'. We will discuss these factors in greater detail.

What currently determines the way we think about public space? The thinking is primarily and significantly influenced by a set notion about the location of public space. Everyone almost automatically thinks that public space refers to specific – urban – locations, such as cafés, squares and parks. For researchers such implicit frameworks are a problem that should not be underestimated. After all, when respondents answer questions they are often guided by these frameworks, implicit or not. This can influence the respondents perception of the actual urban experience to such an extent that the research essentially confirms the pre-existing view, but provides no information about other potential urban experiences in the public space (see, for example, Gadet 1999).

On the lookout

In order to answer our pivotal question about the role of design and strategy in the development of public domain, we must first seek out what constitutes publicness now. Do the large public spaces in the city actually function as public domain? Which other unexpected places possibly manifest themselves as a public domain? We will tackle these questions in the first part of the essay, in which we will concentrate on the cultural geography of the new society.

The search for the public domain is not only a question of the identification of places that might function as public domain. This cultural geography also needs explanation. In which force-fields does the public space take shape? And how is this force-field reflected in current design strategy? Using the concept of the new cultural geography formulated here, as well as new insights into the way in which public space is produced, we will then consider the implicit cultural policy that is adopted in the design of the public space in more detail. Is there reason to talk of a deterioration of the public space or not? Is the sacrifice of authenticity the problem, or is this merely based on a superficial reading of the new publicness? This discussion leads us to the definition of a number of elements for a new cultural programme of requirements for the public space. In the third section we will attempt to formulate the design task for the public domain more accurately on the basis of this cultural programme, and we will outline a set of design instruments with which this task might be tackled.

Schiphol
Nederlandse Spoorwegen
Amsterdam Airport Schipho
Schiphol Plaza
NEE
SCHIPHOL de LUCHT IN, VLIEGTUIGEN AAN DE GROND!
VLIEGANGST HOUE ZO
DE GROENEN

2

The New Cultural Geography

Public domain and the pull of the periphery

If one goes in search of the public domain, one is still referred to the city. The squares, parks, boulevards and streets of the inner city are a model for urban openness. The periphery is situated outside the old city. The 'urban sprawl': a banal collection of little suburban housing estates and industrial zones, always filled in with places with appellations such as 'office parks', 'leisure centres', 'shopping malls' and 'theme parks', illustrate the curious relationship between city and periphery. Thanks to its amorphousness, the periphery arouses heated reactions. It is regarded as the antithesis of the civilized, the cultured, which is automatically associated with the cities as if a given. We also encounter this in discussions about design. In planning and urbanism, the unbridled growth of the periphery constitutes the central problem. Though the periphery has indeed been 'citified', it is not 'urban', nor urbanized: 'zwar verstädtert, jedoch noch nicht urbanisiert', as the German critic Walter Prigge described it (1989, p. 11). It therefore still offers scope for spatial planning and urban design strategies that are intended to 'urbanize' its formlessness. Examples of this can be found everywhere, whether in the transformation of old industrial areas in the periphery of Barcelona or in the restructuring of residential areas like those in the periphery of Berlin, where the large-scale 'Plattenbausiedlungen' from the era of the German Democratic Republic are being redeveloped according to the urban development principles of the 'Planwerk Innenstadt'.

However, the periphery is not simply 'non-city'. It has a much more forceful and independent power than is reflected in the city–periphery dichotomy. A first indication of this is the magnetism of the periphery: it draws all kinds of civic functions, residents and jobs away from the city.

△ Museumplein (Museum Square), Amsterdam

This is sufficiently familiar. In purely spatial terms the peripheral situation now appears to be much more strategic than it was in the past. In many cases the strategic location is determined by 'accessibility' rather than 'centrality'.

However, the second manifestation of the power of the periphery is much more subtle: the cities are increasingly applying the design and control principles of the periphery. It is the ultimate paradox: while urban planners strive to correct the formlessness of the periphery by 'urbanizing' it, in their attempts to regenerate the inner cities they adopt the organizational principles of the periphery. The residential enclave, or gated communities, the 'business park' and the specialized 'shopping mall' demonstrate how living, working, shopping and entertainment in the periphery are made attractive through homogenization, privatization and thematization. In response to the pull of the periphery, its design and control principles are simply copied in the city. Parts of the city are adapted to fit the requirements of wealthy house-hunters and consumers who want a safe, controlled and segregated environment. Paradoxically enough, the attempts to use the authenticity of the inner city to improve its appeal lead to the city centres being thematized, adapted to the supposed expectations of consumers, those seeking entertainment, and tourists. In the final analysis, the future of the European city seems to lie in the consistent design of its centre as a recreational park for the globetrotting tourist, as the British architecture critic Deyan Sudjic described it (1995).

24

Respectable visitors to Salzburg dutifully follow the little 'park & ride' signs that bring them directly to one of the most beautiful multistorey carparks in Europe. In the Mönchberg that divides Salzburg in two, the city council has hewn an enormous carpark with no fewer than six storeys. You drive in from one side in your car, ascend the spiral ramp until you have found a parking space, and after a short ride in a hitech lift you step out into the open air on the other side of the Mönchberg as a pedestrian. You drive in via streets where pedestrians, cars and lorries jostle for space, and walk out into the midst of the magnificence of the old 'Bürgerstadt' of Salzburg. Gothic, late Renaissance and Baroque architecture compete for aesthetic supremacy in what tourist brochures describe as 'The Rome of the North'. The visiting urban planner begins to water at the mouth on seeing the astonishing way that one square opens out into another, at the contrast between the dark Medieval streets and the flashing beams of sunlight that illuminate them, and the endless succession of astounding vistas of new facades, fountains, galleries and arcades.

Salzburg is Europe's answer to Disneyland.

Perhaps the future of the European city really does lie in the consistent design(ing) of the city centre as a leisure park for the tourist, as Sudjic suggested. Salzburg presents itself as an Erholungsausflug from modern life and in terms of cultural-political strategy is utterly consistent with the policy of the big amusement parks. In Salzburg's old Bürgerstadt tourists can lose themselves in daydreams about Mozart's Salzburg or mellifluous memories of Julie Andrews in The Sound of Music, according to taste. The cultural policy in Salzburg's Bürgerstadt is an acknowledgement of certain phenomena, sometimes typically urban, as a hindrance to the stimulation of economic growth (such as mixed zoning, overlapping social environments, or the ethics of urban restraint). Simultaneously the policy recognizes that there are other elements, sometimes not present initially, that are the key to success: controllability, predictability, and the functionalization of the urban space for one specific purpose: consumption by tourists.

The application of the amusement-park discourse to the city brings to life exactly that which Michael Sorkin most dreaded in the ascendancy of amusement parks: 'The amusement park presents its jolly regulated vision of pleasure as a substitute for the democratic public space, and succeeds in doing this by ridding the city of its sting: the presence of the poor, of crime, dirt and work. In the "public" space of the amusement park or the covered shopping centre, even the freedom of speech is limited: there are no demonstrations in Disneyland' (Sorkin 1992, p. xv).

The traffic-free inner city, the strictly controlled cityscape and the policy of revitalization, and the active dream-machine, for example in the guise of little trips in calèches, perhaps with slightly tipsy coachmen in Renaissance costumes, make Salzburg a perfect city for tourist consumption. The tourist leaves the stress of the ever-accelerating society behind in the spiral of the carpark and experiences the entrance into the old Bürgerstadt as a timewarp. It is a simulacrum of an early urban space, complete with cobble stones and devoid of neon advertising and asphalt, with stately coffee houses, and boutiques with buffed parquet floors and window-blinds of stretched toile. Exactly as the British sociologist John Urry described, here you can observe how consumption has for a long time no longer been limited to the familiar touristy consumer goods, such as 'Mozartkugeln' or other chocolate delights. Here the coffee houses, restaurants and theatres, even an entire city centre, are mobilized for tourist consumption (Urry 1995). When you reflect on the development of Salzburg's old Bürgerstadt as typification of an ideal, there is only one difference between a traditional amusement park and a tourist city such as Salzburg: for Disneyland you pay an admission fee as you enter; in Salzburg you pay when you leave the carpark.

The outlook is alarming: the public domain can evidently not exist without the cities, yet within the cities the attempts to save the city centre threaten the very essence of the public domain. Homogenization and thematization sit uncomfortably with the concept of spaces that attract

a wide variety of people and facilitate or allow an exchange between different groups. What remains is just a canned specimen of pure public domain, protected and museum-like, and thus no more than a lifeless imitation of vital public domain.

A different perspective

The pessimism that overshadows many discussions about public space is a direct consequence of the artificial dichotomy between centre and periphery. If one forgets this dichotomy and takes a fresh look, one sees a different picture. If we regard city and periphery as a single urban field then we discover countless places that perhaps form the new public domains that we are seeking. This simultaneously brings new problems to the fore that demand clarification. The urban field is no longer the domain of a civic openness, as the traditional city was, but the territory of a middle-class culture, characterized by increasing mobility, mass consumption and mass recreation. This middle-class culture forces us to look at space in a different way: we not only have to pay more attention to the new spaces that are created for this mass consumption and recreation, but also to the way in which individuals assemble their city for themselves from a whole variety of elements and locations in the urban field. This offers a different perspective on the creation and the design of the public domain.

The contradistinction between city and periphery has in fact been problematic for much longer. As early as 1974, the French geographer Lefebvre wrote that we must not attach too much significance to dichotomies such as 'urban' versus 'rural'. Modern society has in fact always been marked by an ongoing general process of urbanization in which spatial and social correspondences between the local and the global, or between centre and periphery, were produced in the same specific way, time and again. Presenting this as a dichotomy is also a moot point from a sociological perspective. 'Not all life is modern; but all modern life is city life,' stated the British sociologist Zygmunt Bauman (1995, p. 126). Even in the most isolated corners of the countryside, people have in that sense become 'urbanites' and they participate in urban pleasures, from musicals like Cats, Cyrano or Starlight Express to shopping for a whole range of foreign culinary products in one of the hundreds of branches of big chain stores. Urban life is no longer tied to the city as a spatial entity.

In the early 1960s, the planner Melvin Webber argued that in the future the city would start to move towards becoming a larger urbanized environment, a 'non-place urban realm', ordered by the specific character of fixed places. The urban would no longer be characterized by physical density and proximity.

This conceptual approach, new at the time, is only gradually filtering through into the political discussion. Using the concepts of the 'network city' or the 'urban network', politicians are tentatively distancing themselves from the notion that the old urban centres constitute the exclusive integration points of spatial, social and cultural developments. More than before, there is acknowledgement of the possibility that the social dynamics will in future occur on the edges of cities and between them. This is where the 'edge cities' are developing, at the hubs of the infrastructural interchanges (Gareau 1991). Others envisage an even greater sprawl, and talk of '100 Mile Cities' (Sudjic 1992).

The proliferation of new terms and concepts can be seen as evidence that an ever larger circle is dissociating itself from the old dichotomy of city and periphery, and is at the same time an expression of the inability to discuss the new spatial reality in a concrete and differentiated manner. No matter how widely adopted concepts such as urban field, urbanized landscape or network city have now become, when we talk about public space we still always discuss the streets and the squares of the historic city centres.

The limitations of the term 'urban field'

The concept of the urban field is extremely restrictive. It denotes a spatial development, but still offers absolutely no sense of the way this new, bigger space is used. The urban field as we experience it now seems to be the 'non-place urban realm' that Webber foresaw four decades ago. It seems to be an undifferentiated 'urban sprawl': a random collection of a few old urban cores, villages, in the midst of suburban residential areas, shopping centres, airports, brainparks, educational institutions, motorways, hotels, railway and metro lines, nature areas, motorway services, discos, museums, amusement parks, recreation areas, country

estates, stadiums, golf courses, distribution centres, 'leisure' facilities, multiplex cinemas and so on.

The frequent appearance of this motley collection of spatial artefacts in reportages, documentaries, music videos, commercials, films and novels, shows how many people consider these elements as the decor of our actual existence. However, that also indicates the lack of a conceptual language in order to think and talk about this new spatial reality in a meaningful and distinctive terms. In the last forty years, there have been developments that once again distinguish the space of the urban field. Motorways, airports, HST stations and landscape qualities produce 'potential differentiation', in a manner of speaking, between points in the urban field. The concepts of 'network city' and 'urban network' ostensibly offer a solution for this conceptual problem. Because of the emphasis that this places on the virtuality of the networks and the transience of the intersections, it still remains unclear how these networks structure the urbanized space.

City centres are no longer necessarily the central core within the field, but as 'condensations' they are comparable with new concentrations, which increasingly exhibit a combination of living, working and 'leisure' facilities, just like the old centres. In order to understand the developments in the urban field, we must know what determines the potential of a particular location. Then it is also easier to understand where spatial planning is going against the flow, and where it seems to be mistakenly overlooking latent strengths or threats.

It is obvious that an important part of the urban dynamism has shifted to the edges of existing cities and that completely new concentrations are developing there. All kinds of things happen at motorway interchanges, at airports, or at points that are attractive for recreation. Considered from a perspective that is based solely on the attractiveness of the inner city, at first glance this seems to constitute a loss. However, there are just as many opportunities for the development of the public domain here. This assumes that the urban field is no longer approached as an undifferentiated space, as a 'non-place urban realm', but rather as a space where in fact a number of 'places' come into being that are different in character. In order to be able to exploit this potential for the development of the public domain there is a need for both an informed cultural strategy and for urban planning concepts that utilize, combine or stimulate the spontaneous developments in an unexpected way. In other words urbanism that is capable of bringing about spatial, social and cultural intersections and interferences. It also means that the inner cities will not be abandoned: the city is not diametrically opposed to the urban field, but is rather a part of it. The attractiveness of the old centres can in fact profit from the diffusion of consumption, recreation and tourism across larger areas of the urban field.

Having already reawakened interest in the cultural significance of the city it is now time to turn the spotlight on the cultural potential of the urban field. The transposition of the urban renewal exercise to the postwar residential areas, the criticism of the monofunctional and monotonous new housing estates, the admission that the increased attractiveness itself forms yet another problem for many inner cities, the spatial claims of large-scale shopping and recreation facilities, the development of 'new nature', and the consequences of the restructuring of agriculture for the countryside are all questions that demand more than a simple functional-spatial analysis.

What is needed first of all is a more precise analysis of the nature of the dynamism. More especially the question of what types of places are presently evolving. What interests us is the cultural 'identity' of the new places, alongside the change in character of the old places, and the potential of these places as public domain.

The cultural geography of the urban field

In order to gain a better understanding of the cultural potentials of the diversity of places in the urban field we must give more thought to the way in which spatial coherence is experienced. We must look for cultural meaning. This is the domain of a cultural geography, a geography that is concerned with the semantics of the spatial. A cultural geography shifts the focus away from the analysis of the functionality of 'spaces' that are quasi-acultural to the space as a system of 'places' with specific meanings for specific groups.

The difference between thinking in terms of 'space' and thinking in terms of 'place' has deep philosophical roots (see Harvey 1989; Casey 1997). As a classification, space is associated with the Enlightenment, the Age of Reason, at which time it denoted emptiness. Space can thus

be arranged in unambiguous rational units. Spatial planning is then a question of development, for example by the elaboration of a functional hierarchy between small cores, medium-size cores, and urban interchanges. 'Place' is a concept that has in fact been used as a criticism of the thinking of the Enlightenment (cf. Keith & Pile 1993, Jameson 1991). Space is not empty and nor does it allow rational infill. Places are, for example, associated with real events (which have taken place there), with myths, with history and memories. It is this very confrontation between thinking in terms of space and thinking in terms of place – often unobserved – that lies at the root of many conflicts about spatial development and the failure of projects for all their good intentions.

Cultural geography addresses the technical and functional-spatial orientation of space and the neglect of a cultural construction of all kinds of places that are imbued with meaning. The pursuit of the actualization of a perfect, logical arrangement is superseded by the analysis of the extant qualities of existing places and the inference of ways in which those qualities can be tapped.

A functional-spatial analysis leaves no room for the many ways in which meanings are etched in the landscape. On the other hand, the increased attention for the cultural meaning of places is generally nostalgic in tone and static by nature. This creates the impression that the only impact of spatial interventions is the loss of meaning. However, interventions can also realize or reveal new meanings. Adriaan Geuze's rearrangement of the central Schouwburgplein (Theatre Square) in Rotterdam created the basis for a new stage-set for various groups of young people who have claimed spots on and around the edges of the square, where they exhibit themselves with their particular lifestyles: breakdancers on the square, the parade of Antillian youngsters driving round the edge of the square in front of De Doelen concert hall and congress centre in their cars on Friday and Saturday evening, groups of young women who cluster together on the long benches opposite the multiplex cinema. This is how a new, dynamic cultural geography evolves, one in which meanings are not fixed but in an ongoing state of flux and development.

The shift towards a cultural-geographic approach involves a departure from the notion of absolutism in ascertaining the value or meaning of spaces. The essence of a cultural geography is precisely that analysis of the am-

The Lijnbaan, conceived and built as a shopping precinct, is a favourite promenade for youngsters from the suburbs. This promenade of young people walking to and fro, to see and be seen, is a time-honoured phenomenon. In the 1930s, big groups of young people, albeit of a different ilk, walked up and down along Groene Hilledijk and the Dreef in the garden-suburb Vreewijk in the evening. The groups of boys and girls basically have plenty to offer each other, and are thus an interesting phenomenon in themselves. Of course this was and still is considered a nuisance by other people. However, in the shopping area their cultural geography rubs up against a different, dominant geography. Shopkeepers think that the youngsters 'don't have any reason to be here'. They don't buy anything and simply hang around.

biguity or, in more political terms, the struggle between various meanings. Designing public domain can then become a question of the stimulation of informal manifestations of diversity and the avoidance of interventions that are intended to make such manifestations impossible.

It is this production of new and meaningful places that interests us in this context. In The Tourist Gaze, John Urry outlines the rise of the 'heritage industry', which increasingly generates its own cultural geography (1990). He has counted more than 700 new British museums over the last two decades. It should be noted here that these museums did not establish themselves, but are usually another crux in the new policy of a particular city, village or region, the so-called 'heritage centres' developed around certain places with a cultural-historical value.

A new cultural geography is also being deliberately constructed outside the immediate sphere of the tourist industry. New museums and theatres are being deployed in a strategy to improve the image of certain city neighbourhoods, a provincial town is planted on the cultural world-map with a catchy slogan ('Amersfoort, City of Mondrian'), or a new suburb is accorded the exalted status of 'country estate'.

The revival of the notion of place thus has a pronouncedly dual character. As soon as a place – whether an inner city, an industrial monument, an historically interesting building, an untouched village green or a characteristic landscape – attracts the attention of the tourist industry, project developers or 'city promoters', it is threatened by expropriation. Cities, buildings and landscapes are adapted to satisfy the 'eye of the tourist' (Urry 1990). The original multitude of meanings is then usually reduced to one: that of the promotional brochure.

The process is a dynamic one, for meanings and uses are always liable to change. Renegotiation of understandings is ongoing; contention accompanies the process' (Goheen 1998).

Seen in this way, both the riot on the Ypenburg 'country estate' and the unexpected (and for some people undesirable) use of the Schouwburgplein in Rotterdam are examples of a struggle about the character of public space. The publicness of these places is not all that threatened by 'youths hanging out' or suspected paedophiles, but it is in fact that very 'exchange' – often intense – that creates public domain. That is the essence of public domain: different groups become attached to a particular place and somehow or other they must reach a compromise. Which codes should dominate there? What behaviour should be tolerated? Who is allowed to ask whom to adapt? These are questions that are part and parcel of meaningful public space.

The examples presented here also make it obvious that the resulting meanings are never the sole defining factor for the character of the new places. Of course some have more impact on the eventual character of new and old places than others: it is not ridiculous to talk in terms of a trend towards commercialization and to question its validity. However, commercialization and the 'market' are not the only forces. From our viewpoint, a cultural-geographic analysis must tackle both the analysis of the production of all kinds of places and the analysis of the specific way in which those places are used or 'consumed', sometimes contrary to the intentions of the producer.

The production of places and 'non-places'

The way in which 'the market' – the economy, globalization, 'neo-liberal hyper-capitalism' – threatens or even destroys the 'authenticity' of the historic meaning of local 'places' has often been a topic of discussion. These viewpoints have little consideration for the creation of scores of valuable new places. The possibility of these being created by 'the market' seems to be peremptorily dismissed. Privatization and commercialization are considered irreconcilable with the concept of public domain, but that discrepancy is less absolute than it might seem.

Firstly, as we have seen, there appears to be a demand for a cultural definition of spaces from various economic sectors. This demand has

increasingly led to the conscious production of meanings, the creation of spheres, and the development of themes. The telecommunications revolution has decreased the number of functionally necessary meetings, but at the same time new and usually higher demands are made of the places where the meetings are held. Influenced by tourism, local history is rediscovered, countless artefacts have sometimes literally been dug up, restored, or even coolly built anew – to an historic plan. Rotterdam's new logo, the Erasmus Bridge, is also part of the new tactic of city councils to use symbols and spheres in their attempts to cement the loyalty of companies and citizens. In the leisure industry, 'places' are created on an assembly line. Center Parcs holiday camps produce the enclaves that make 'a wonderful weekend away' a sure success. The Royal Dutch Touring Club (ANWB) oversees the tourist corridors for motorists, cyclists and hikers: 'Ontdek je plekje,' is one of their slogans that roughly translates as 'Discover your ideal spot.'

The landscape of old is being converted into the new at a rapid tempo. But what kind of landscape is this, from a cultural-geographic perspective? What is the character of all these newly created 'places' and routes? How are they interrelated? What happens there, who partakes in the life at those new places, and how? To what extent is there a question of exchange or interaction between different groups? In short, just how 'urban' is the urban field?

The French anthropologist Marc Augé made an important but controversial contribution to this discussion a few years ago. In effect he turns the argument on its head: at the moment it is not a case of the development of new 'places' that leads to the continuation of urban life at other locations. On the contrary, the new 'places' lack the essential characteristics that would make it possible to actually call them places. In this respect he is also talking about 'non-places', which are dominated by their transitory character (where people do not repose, but at best pass time) and thus in fact contradict the notion of place.

Augé also applies a discourse analysis and examines the terms in which these new transit spaces are described: 'Places and non-places are opposed (or attracted) like the words and notions that enable us to describe them. But the fashionable words... are associated with non-places. Thus we can contrast the realities of transit (transit camps or passengers in transit) with those of residence or dwelling; the interchange (where nobody crosses anyone else's path) with the crossroads (where people meet); the passenger (defined by his destination) with the traveller (who strolls along his route). Significantly, the SNCF still calls its customers travellers until they board the TGV; then they become passengers), the housing estate ('group of dwellings', Larousse says), where people do not live together and which is never situated in the centre of anything (big estates characterize the so-called peripheral zones of outskirts), with the monument where people share and commemorate; communication (with its codes, images and strategies) with language (which is spoken)' (Augé 1995, pp. 107-108).

In summary, places are marked by identity, social relations and history, while non-places have no identity and are difficult to define in social or historical terms: 'The space of non-place creates neither singular identity nor relations; only solitude, and similitude' (Augé 1995, p. 103).

Augé's work has been extremely influential in the study of these transit spaces. However, it is highly questionable whether his analysis of non-places does justice to the way in which these spaces are actually used. Augé notes that the possibility of becoming a non-place threatens each and every place. But can it work the other way round, and can non-places become places? The theory of non-places does not answer this question. It once again illustrates that on a conceptual level we do not know what to do when it comes to these new spaces outside the familiar urban public domains.

Besides noting the corridor-like character of the so-called non-places, Augé points out two other aspects that play an important role in the dismissal of these new spaces: the private character and the lack of authenticity. The spaces that Augé refers to are not just transit spaces, but are also usually privatized and thus are not public spaces in the strict sense. For many people this is reason to disregard them as possible public domains.

Another point that Augé touches on concerns the lack of authenticity of the new spaces. The criticism of the thematized and controlled worlds of 'fantasy city' is that it creates a pseudo-world that is presented as a substitute for the democratic urban domain. The exclusion of the dangers and irritations of urban life goes hand in hand with the eradication of the unexpected and the spontaneous, which are just as characteristic a feature of urban life. Synthetic experiences replace historic, social and cultural meanings. This preclusion of what cannot be controlled almost automatically leads to the exclusion of certain uses and behaviour, and eventually the exclusion of certain groups.

We must take the alarm bells that these analyses and criticisms sound extremely seriously: warnings about the decline in openness, the exclusion of specific groups from life in public, and the curtailment of essential civil rights, such as the right to demonstrate. Nevertheless, an analysis of the new urban landscape that deals exclusively with commercialization, lack of authenticity, control and exclusion, is inadequate.

The Barcelona architect and urbanist Manuel de Solá-Morales, for example, has correctly pointed out that such an analysis skims over the way that these non-public but still collective spaces sometimes actually function. De Solá-Morales broached the argument that the fixation on the true public spaces of the city leads to the disregard for everything else that is developing in terms of collectively used spaces, both in the city and its periphery. Here he is also referring to railway, metro and bus stations, airports, shopping malls, discos, amusement parks – spaces that are not public in the strict sense, but are experienced by most people as important public spaces. In his view, the urbanist's task cannot be limited to the design of the public spaces, but must be broadened to include the integration of public spaces and those indistinct privatized spaces into a system of urban collective spaces. As an antidote to the fear for the privatization of the public domain he presents the possibility of urbanizing private domains, or the integration of the private in the sphere of the public. The simple fact that something is not completely public is no reason to dismiss the location as public domain.

There are also various things to counter the argument of the lack of authenticity. Urry endorses a quote from the cultural anthropologist MacCannell that where we can talk of authenticity in most cases it concerns 'staged authenticity' (Urry 1990, p. 9). And in the final chapter of Fantasy City, Hannigan writes: '"Fruitopian communities" – restored urban areas organized around festival market places and the like – may be closer to stage sets than real streetscapes, but even a Fruitopian Town is better

An example of a successful approach to collective space as potential public domain is the foyer of the Academisch Ziekenhuis (University Hospital) in Groningen. A new hallway was added to this Moloch, which serves as home to numerous everyday functions and facilities. People from the adjacent neighbourhoods come here for the post office, a cup of coffee, or a newspaper. En passant, it has created the sphere of exchange and interaction that typifies public domain.

than a placeless suburbia where there is no town to go to at all' (1998, p. 197).

Hammering on critically about the manageability aspect also demands a more refined approach. Ignoring the fairly generally held feeling of insecurity will only encourage the flight from the 'real' public space to the safe and synthetic world of the pseudo-public spaces.

This indicates that a cultural-geographic analysis of the production of places and non-places should also include an analysis of the consumption of these new places and non-places. The way that spatial interrelationships are perceived and experienced and the way that the cultural meanings of places are produced, is not simply determined by their developers and designers, but to a similar extent by the consumers. It is in this very association that we can perhaps attain a more realistic view of the meaning of these new spaces as public domain. Why do people go to the new places? What role do they play in the organization of people's daily lives and the building of a way of life?

Place as a consumer good

Recent years have seen an unprecedented increase in interest for the deliberate consumption of places and 'events'. That is a consequence of the substantial expansion of the middle class in developed countries. Influenced by this ever more dominant middle class, there are at least two related trends that have become prominent in the cultural geography of the urban field: the conscious consumption of 'cultural' experiences and the conscious avoidance of the confrontations with the proverbial 'other' in daily life. These two trends seem to be seamlessly aligned, but in reality they are at odds with each other. Isn't the pursuit of the confrontation with what is 'other' or 'foreign' the ultimate cultural experience? The tension between the two trends is especially important for our search for the public domain.

A phenomenon that has mushroomed in recent years concerns the desire of the ordinary citizen to have 'interesting' experiences. Leisure experts talk about an 'experience market', where all kinds of events are offered that can excite people for a short time, from factory sales to art biennials. We can find an example of the conscious consumption of places

in cultural tourism. Cities and organizations compete with other places by producing experiences. The success of exhibitions is currently measured by the degree to which they are an 'event', i.e. develop into mass crowd-pullers of international importance.

The mass cultural consumption indicates how the definition of places is directly related to the mobilization of cultural heritage with the orchestrated production and marketing of cultural events. But this production of experiences and 'events' only functions thanks to the urge for social and cultural mobility: the fact that people develop an identity by attending this kind of event or place. Being present or sharing in this deserves a high-lighted entry in one's personal biography (see Hitzler 1988; Hitzler & Honer 1994). Whoever is able to secure a ticket not only has access to the exhibition, but also, it would seem, has gained admission to a cultural elite and a building block of a lifestyle shared with them. People also turn out to be exceptionally mobile in the spatial sense, in order to participate in this collective congestion. Typically, they then bemoan the 'growing' popularity. As yet, they refuse to acknowledge that the putative cultural elite itself became a mass a long time ago (see Bell 1978).

In a certain sense, the popular focus on the consumption of experiences is a worry for metropolitan administrators and entrepreneurs. The unstoppable demand for new and different experiences means that producers have to continually update and revise their 'formula'. Nowadays, city centres are given a facelift every so many years to answer to new consumer preferences. Amusement parks have to continually innovate

◁ Former corn exchange, West Sussex, Great Britain

The big Paul Cézanne exhibition in Paris in 1995 attracted 632,956 visitors. The French press agency AFP reported that the Cézanne retrospective was thus the fifth most success-ful exhibition in the Grand Palais. Since 1985, the record had been held by Renoir (789,764 visitors), followed by Monet (735,207), Gauguin (623,739), and Toulouse-Lautrec (653,853). The big Rembrandt exhibition, the Expo in Seville, the 100th anniversary of the Biennale in Venice, the 350,000 visitors who came to see 22 Vermeer paintings in the Mauritshuis in The Hague, the big Goya exhibition that was meant to 'make' the Spanish tourist season of 1996: congestion is the proof of success in a cultural industry focused on the production of 'events'. The exhibition of the Barnes Collection in the Haus der Kunst in Munich was so popular that the museum decided to keep the exhi-bition open at night for the final weeks. However, this did not help to channel the stream of visitors one bit, because this nocturnal visit to the exhibition was dis-covered as an 'event' in its own right.

in order to keep pace, and museums are forced to curate exhibitions with catchy themes in order to reach their visitor targets. But the consumer is unpredictable. When places become too slick, when they focus too much on the supposed desires of the consumer, they become predictable and their attraction to the critical consumer as an experience diminishes.

The individual importance that people attach to attending cultural events in the city is at odds with their fear for certain other negative forms of urban congestion. The patterns of this avoidance of congestion is in fact just as important in defining the cultural geography. Sociologist Ulrich Beck (1986, 1993) thinks that the most important change in modern society right now lies in the displacement of social conflicts about the distribution of 'goods' to those about the distribution of 'bads', supposed or actual. In the final decades of the 20th century, society was forced to deal with the inadvertent by-products of modernization. New social conflicts often revolve around the sharing of the negative aspects of modernization, such as rubbish dumps, crime, new infrastructure (from HST routes to airport runways and motorways), asylum-seeker centres, or sheltered facilities for drug addicts.

The consumption of space in the urban field is thus on the one hand focused on the massive increase in 'events' and positive places, and on the other, the equally massive avoidance of all kinds of negative aspects of social progress. When people go shopping or go out on the town they want to be entertained, not alarmed. In the sphere of the home, we see a growing tendency towards creating a distance from the urban problems and the groups associated with them. All this indicates that the growing middle class primarily uses the urban field in order to separate itself along social lines, and that an exchange between different social groups occurs less often.

The urban field as an archipelago of enclaves

Based on the analysis of production and consumption of places and non-places above, we can arrive at a cultural-geographic interpretation of the spatial term 'urban field'. Society has become an archipelago of enclaves, and people from different backgrounds have developed ever more effective spatial strategies to meet the people they want to meet, and to avoid the people they want to avoid (see also Hajer & Halsema 1997; Reijndorp

▷ Dance Valley, the Netherlands

et al. 1998). On the level of the urban field it is possible to distinguish between countless monocultural enclaves, from gated communities to business parks, from recreational woodlands to golf courses. Furthermore, there are countless non-places at this level: non-territorial spaces such as motorways, airports, industrial areas, stations, railway lines and distribution hubs that are designed functionally. Indeed, viewed objectively, non-places could just as easily be considered places, though they display the features of functionalism and are acultural.

How can we explain the emergence of this archipelago of enclaves? Using the work of Manuel Castells we can place this cultural geography of the urban field in a broader framework. He considers the new thinking in terms of 'place' in the context of the emergence of the 'network society'. In the network society, the traditional city is swallowed up in an irregular urban landscape. An enormous leap in the level of mobility is coupled with the scattering of activities, which leads to a new urban form. This new metropolitan form actually connects the urban, the rural and the suburban environments. The result is a network, a seemingly structureless conglomeration of functions. Nobody developed this metropolis: it simply comes into being. In the new cultural geography everyone creates their own city for themselves, a combination of the various places that are important for that individual.

There are two sides to this individualized spatial planning. On the one hand there is a growing supply of monofunctional and generally culturally and socially homogenous enclaves: residential districts, office parks, shopping centres and amusement parks. Each individual constructs his or her own city from these geographically dispersed enclaves. Just like the traditional city, that individual city can include safe and less safe zones, more or less homogenous places. There are still people who opt for the social heterogeneity and cultural diversity of the city. But for many people the decline in the quality of the surroundings, the lack of safety and the inconvenience are enough to tip the scales towards an individual city that is as far as possible constructed from a combination of carefully selected, safe, socially homogenous places which can be reached easily, safely and comfortably by car. People can apparently still be urbanites while not necessarily residing in the city.

This leads to the archipelago structure that we have described. Nobody would want to refuse people the right to decide where they want to live.

56

At the same time, it is obvious that a great deal of mobility has to be understood as a 'mobility of avoidance'. If possible, the 'socially mobile' citizen moves to a house outside the city. An often heard argument is that the city is not an environment where you can raise a child. And it is obvious that this not only pertains to the physical environment, but also and primarily to the social. A garden is nice, but the 'white school' is probably more important. This is how a 'structural heterogeneity' in society, which is more often manifest in the degree and the way that people relocate, is formed. The cultural-geographic map is one of themed and condensed places connected by a network of motorways and railways. The archipelago is built up from a multitude of different microcosmic worlds that can still be reached via a convenient station or motorway slip-road. This gives the urban field the character of an 'ecology of fantasy' (Crawford 1988), which is defined by the principles of the theme park: thematization and concentration. There is not one single environment that is immune to this urge to give everything a theme, whether a restaurant, business, park or residential area.

One example is the renewal of the city parks in the city of Groningen – a trendsetter as far as the revitalization of the public space is concerned – in which each park was given a theme that is a reference to a particular lifestyle.

The motorway makes it possible to travel directly from one themed environment to another. The in-between spaces simply fly past. This compression does not simply amalgamate physically distant places into a single space, but also ostracizes certain places, for example parts of the city that have a bad reputation based on TV images or newspaper reports. This is an impression that will not be amended, because people do not even consider going there. Unless these parts of the city also develop an attraction value, are given a theme: a deprived neighbourhood packaged as an exotic environment where people go on 'safari'.

The development outlined here obviously does not unfold in a quasi-natural fashion. It is nonsense to argue that in the face of these developments

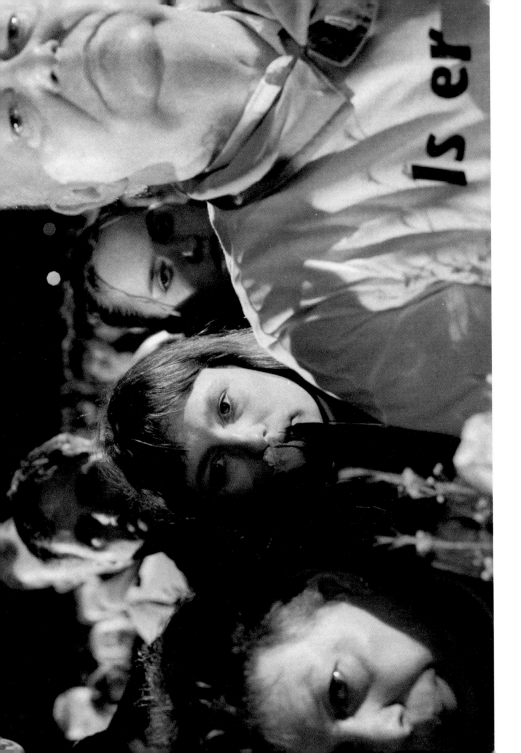

there can no longer be any such thing as spatial policy. Choices are continually being made – spatial design included – that reinforce or facilitate some processes, while slowing down others or making them impossible. There is simply insufficient consideration for this socio-cultural dynamic in the urban field, or the only response is in moral-political rather that instrumental terms. The question should not be how to hold back this transformation into an archipelago but rather what possibilities this new spatial and social reality offers for the creation of new and interesting forms of public domain. A clue to how to answer this question can be found in the ambivalent attitude of many inhabitants of the urban field towards the homogeneity and the predictability of the selection of places from which they can compose their city. After all, they are seeking adventures and experiences that are not so conspicuously pre-programmed.

The archipelago of enclaves does not develop without conflict. The spatial organization or reorganization that is currently occurring obviously elicits new social conflicts. Castells (1996) sees a confrontation between a culture of local 'places' and the international culture of the 'space of flows': 'What is distinctive of new social structure, the network society, is that most dominant processes, concentrating power, wealth, and information, are organized in the space of flows. Most human experience, and meaning, are still locally based.' Here Castells seems to be reserving 'place' for the reaction to what was previously called 'anonimization'. He notes the development of the struggle between processes of increases in scale ('space of flows') and the socio-cultural reaction to this (the defence of the 'space of places'). In this manner, the search for new public domain could be seen in terms of a struggle between places and non-places. But this approach is in fact overly schematic. Firstly, at this point in time, places are being produced in massive quantities. The Walt Disney Corporation developed the 'little city' known as Celebration on the basis of the terms 'community', 'education', 'communication' and 'place'. What the activities of the Disney Corporation and the British 'heritage industry' mentioned above, as well as the Ypenburg example, make clear is that there is a raging battle over this 'space of places'. In some cases places are defended against the forces of the 'space of flows', but in other cases places are not so much defended as staged. We observe the development of a 'new collectivity', the creation of new collective forms of housing with fashionable titles such as 'country estates' and 'residential parks', or provocative slogans such as 'camping country'. The 'space of flows' and the 'space of places' are both actors in the cultural geography of the urban field.

An important result of this approach is that the cultural geography of the urban field is not dictated by material or typological qualities. The urban field that people create for themselves is at least as much a function of fears and anxieties, ambitions and dreams, of views about society, the relationship with nature, and what constitutes a 'good life'. This environment is where the battle for public space is fought.

The formation of archipelagos and public domain: consequences for the analysis

The cultural-geographic approach exchanges the terms 'space' and 'distance' for thinking in terms of 'movement' and 'experienced time'. People and businesses make choices, the government reacts, and a new cultural geography is born in this process. This cannot be deduced from the functional typology, but requires a more specific analysis of the meanings that people attribute to places.

What does this approach offer for the way we think about public space? Our cultural-geographic approach to the urban field distances itself from the unremittingly negative discussion about non-places and about the commercialization or militarization of public spaces, or the lack of 'authenticity'. The analysis of the Netherlands as an archipelago of enclaves indicates that the socio-cultural segregation in the Netherlands proceeds unabated. In the debate about the potential for public domain this forms a given. In a certain sense this brings the basic problem into even sharper focus: Is it still possible to discover or develop places in the archipelago of enclaves that interest a broad assortment of groups and where an exchange between these groups occurs?

The above will have simultaneously made clear that we believe that the new cultural geography does not simply allow an analysis of socio-cultural segregation. The same analysis shows that this process in no way unfolds straightforwardly or without conflict.

Firstly, we see locations that actually function as public domain, albeit often in unexpected places. This establishes a new topography of old and new public places. We can also identify locations that could develop into

public domain because of their design and prevailing policy. The key to the public domain then lies in the analysis of the 'experienced time' at specific places and the link with a design or policy objective. In future, the quality of public domain will not merely be measured in terms of space and accessibility, but will increasingly become a question of how it influences the ambience of specific places.

Secondly, the urbanite is perhaps too often characterized as an 'Etui-Mensch' who has withdrawn from the confusion and menace of metropolitan life, travelling to places that are as homogenous and free of strange blemishes as his own living environment within the protective cocoon of his private car. Although people and businesses do consciously seek out enclaves, the attitude of many people with regards to these homogenous and themed environments is in fact much more ambivalent than is often suggested (Reijndorp et al. 1998). People live in an enclave because they are starting a family, but at the same time take an emphatic part in the urban life beyond its boundaries; people work in an office district, but miss the very urbanity of their former workplace; people visit the amusement park, but value precisely those moments when the complete stage management of space and behaviour encounters a hitch.

Those who take the development of de-urbanization as a given run the risk of adding to it through design. On the other hand, those who take note of the ambivalence of citizens, governments and businesses, and dare to consider the motives behind certain actions, create a prospect for a new task for design and policy. The starting point for this is the fact that all the actors continually make conscious decisions without in fact having full freedom of choice. The faltering of the naturalness that is rooted in age-old traditions forces the modern urbanite, the inhabitant of the urban field, to continually make choices (Giddens 1994). Daily life may to a large degree amount to routine, but individuals still attach a personal interpretation to what they do. What's more, in this context the place of residence is no longer predictable. The fact that someone does not live in a city does not necessarily mean that someone is not an urbanite. The fact that someone books an organized holiday does not necessarily mean that someone is a run-of-the-mill tourist. Opting for a particular domicile in a particular location is not driven solely by practical considerations; it also forms a statement in the life-story that people create for and about themselves. This story contains contradictions, and for some of these narratives this is the essential characteristic: people present them-

64

selves as pragmatists or conceive their own lives as that of a 'bricoleur'. People are able to recognize the limitations of a chosen option and still defend it.

People put together a lifestyle, as it were, from the components on offer. In this, some seek more coherence and consistency, while others – such as the 'bricoleur' – opt for contrast and for modules that may not seem to fit together.

The space of the inhabitant of the urban field – whether living in the city, a suburb or a village – is shaped by the urbanized landscape, wherein different places take on different meanings in everyday life. Each puts together his own polycentric urban area and thus creates a new form of urbanity that is characterized more by agility than by movement. The new urbanity thus reflects the new, highly dynamic 'time-space patterns' of citizens: increasing flexibility in the world of employment, changes in the form of personal relationships, shared responsibilities in the home, cultural trends in home life and recreation.

Because private life is so complicated it increasingly seeps through into the public sphere. Urban resources such as restaurants and bistros make it possible for greater groups to allocate their time-space budget more efficiently. The flourishing growth of the 'city for going out' is unmistakable, and terrace after terrace is laying claim on the public space.

It is important to note that the 'individual' organization of the space is not as individual as the term might imply. Specific locations are appropriated by what Manuel de Solá-Morales has described as 'urban tribes', characterized by a shared interest. In other respects the members of such a 'tribe' can be different to each other. This subjects the meaning of places in the urban field to significant change. Places can go from being 'in' for certain groups to being 'out' again. That ephemeral quality is reinforced by the exponential growth in the use of mobile telephones. 'Meeting' is less and less a matter of coincidence or one based on the routine of regularly visited haunts (the local pub); it is being organized at any given time at any given place via the mobile. This is increasingly turning the public and collective space of the urban field into a space in which various small 'tribes' wander about and claim their territory.

Essential to our approach to the challenge of the public domain at this juncture is that we believe that this analysis of the palette of individual choices, and especially the fact that people in this context adopt ambiv-

alent attitudes as regards what they do, is at odds with the way in which the space is prestructured at present. Spaces are being prestructured for certain modes of behaviour, which allows no opportunity for the very diversity and ambivalence we have identified as regards the enclave culture. But perhaps the need, or even the desire, for monoculturalism has been overestimated, while in fact design and policy can conceivably establish links between the environments of different groups of users that will not lead to conflict and trouble. The combination of 'VINEX locations' (new housing areas primarily consisting of single-family dwellings, usually built as an 'add-on' development on the edge of existing urban boundaries) with public domain is not inconceivable, and nor are urban experiences in and around theme parks.

When everyone is creating an individual, polycentric urban area it is precisely in the 'experienced time' that the challenges for a new public domain lie. Public domain may well come into being where places re-present multiple and incongruent meanings. Between ten and eleven o'clock at night, the Leidseplein in Amsterdam is public domain. The Stadsschouwburg and the Balie theatres empty, films end and begin, the early night-owls begin to arrive, restaurant customers gradually file out onto the square. While tourists watch the street artists – often from abroad, just as they are – people seem to share the compressed space without sharing much common meaning. But it is precisely this multiplicity and incongruence that makes the square into public domain at this hour. Who are those others? Why are they here? What are their dreams and what are their lifestyles? Perhaps that is also why the London Underground counts as an extraordinary example of public domain. Because practically everyone in London is dependent on the Underground for transport during the rush hour and late at night, here you see a platform with travellers of extremely varied sorts. The very sharing of the platform makes exchange possible between groups that otherwise follow entirely separate time-space paths. Oddly enough this also applies for little café terraces such as 'Le Petit Pain' at Schiphol Airport's Plaza. The variety of public that makes use of this spot is greater than at any traditional civic square. From families waving off their son at the start of his trip around the world to migrants exchanging experiences, from shoppers at the mall to account managers from the surrounding offices. Surprisingly, there are also remarkably few barriers to exclude the homeless here.

The cultural-geographic approach shows that the 'public domain' concept is not in the least out-of-date. Its manifestation may be something quite different from the traditional public space of the city.

△ Roger van Boxtel (Minister for Urban Policy and Integration of Ethnic Minorities) and actress Isa Hoes open a violence-free zone, Amsterdam

3

△ Saftlevenkwartier (Saftleven neighbourhood), Rotterdam

Public Space and Cultural Policy

The design and spatial organization of the public space tell us a lot about cultural ambitions. They illustrate cherished wishes and innate desires. The layout and appearance of the public space can also tell a tale of fear, uncertainty and neglect. We can 'read' the street like this. Decisions about the way that the public space will be filled in are an expression of the way we deal with the shaping of the society. By arranging or rearranging the physical forms of the space, or by intervening in the 'programme' of public places, we create new opportunities for particular activities or groups and we possibly reduce the chances for other uses or other groups. The re-design of a number of small parks in Manhattan resulted in the repression of all sorts of processes by which certain groups appropriate the limited space: previously the public quality of these park squares had been eroded because the only people who still making use of it were groups of youths, dog-owners and the homeless. Thanks to the introduction of a strict subdivision into different spheres the parks once more became attractive for a greater diversity of visitors. But we also make cultural policy through types of design, or through opting for a certain 'theme' (see also Hajer & Halsema 1997). Of course the cultural-political significance of these decisions is not always explicitly acknowledged, nor is it always intended to be. In many cases this means there is also a question of an 'implicit' cultural policy. In this section we want to reconstruct the cultural policy as regards the public space, both in its implicit manifestations and in the instances when it is a matter of a more explicit cultural policy.

In the mid-1960s, the Council of Europe published a series of brochures about urban cultural policy. Faced with the deathly dullness of the new urban environments that were designed in the 1960s, the Council of Europe put forward suggestions for a policy to revitalize the city centres and residential districts. In the light of the hushed chill of the recently built British New Towns, the Swedish satellite towns and the Dutch growth cores, the emergence of this need for revitalization is easily appreciated. In various countries the suggestions led to initiatives by the national governments to put the cultural-political dimension of city expansion and urban planning on the agenda. In the Netherlands, for example, the Ministry of Culture brought out the memorandum De recreatieve stad ('The Recreational City', 1979). This called attention to the 'podium function' of the city long before the spatial planners had discovered culture as an important factor in the economic regeneration of the city.

Alongside the dullness and the monofunctionality of many new urban areas, the somewhat older cultural-political theme of cultural 'blandening' formed an important consideration in the suggestions of the Council of Europe. What had become known in the postwar years as the problem of the man in the crowd, characterized by a passive and consumptive attitude, was now trotted onto the stage cloaked in the guise of 'consumer culture'. The aim was not only the revitalization of the urban space, but also the promotion of the active involvement of large sections of the population in the urban culture, and the creation of new opportunities for personal development: 'A cultural policy is effective when it enables the average man to validate the uniqueness of his personality in a society which threatens constantly to thrust him into anonymity, facelessness and impotence' (Simpson 1976, p. 36).

The core thinking was that the public space of the cities had to be animated. 'Animation policy' was developed to this end and special 'animators' were appointed. 'The task of the animators is to stimulate and cultivate this participation. Their activities take myriad forms. Theatre groups perform on the street or in the factory. Librarians lure people to their libraries by making them into centres for general social life.... A guideline for each animator is Edgar Faure's remark: "First and foremost it is necessary to create a need for culture." By presenting people with forms of experience, they endeavour to enable them to recognize and express needs that were until now unconscious' (Mennell 1976, p. 18).

The public space was viewed as a place where people could pick up new ideas and find their way to all sorts of cultural institutions and initiatives. Although somewhat ambivalent, this new approach was not ruled by an exalted view of culture. The animation strategy was carried out under the banner of cultural pluralism. That is not to say that every 'cultural' expression was considered equally valid. Cultural development and cultural participation were given primacy as a response to the blandening tendencies of the 'consumer culture'. 'Cultural pluralism does not mean a laissez-aller acceptance of every manifestation of life. This would be to cut away the ground from under the feet of any cultural intervention. Tolerance is not extended – and here conviction comes to the aid of reason – to that passive, consumer "culture" which is sprayed over the populace by the mass media and commercial entertainment. No culture which involves people in passivity is authentic.... In so far as television does not provide a stimulus to critical participation, in so far as it is a mere adjunct of domestic comfort, a form of receptivity and relaxation, it is not a part of any culture' (Mennell 1976, p. 37).

Looking back, it is remarkable to what extent the cultural policy was ruled by the battle against the dull and the bland. It was an era in which participating cities such as Bologna, Italy, and the Dutch provincial town of Apeldoorn were growing rapidly, and cultural facilities lagged behind. Society was becoming increasingly characterized by consolidation and uniformity, and the policy aimed to fight the cultural poverty that was the inevitable result. The street was the gateway to Culture: thanks to the street and open-air theatre more people would supposedly find their way to the museums, the concert halls, the theatres and the libraries.

The animation strategy of the Council of Europe was a form of explicit cultural policy that now appears dated in more than one respect. This may not apply so much to the attempts to call a halt the cultural blandening. Even today, critics of 'fast-food culture' and commercialization trumpet their part in the debate about urban culture and public space. But as far as vitality goes, the animation strategy seems to have more than succeeded. These days it forms a standard part of the cultural strategy of just about every city. The parade of passers-by, the terrace culture, the new museums, the reprofiled squares, the cinema complexes, the rediscovery of the opera, the Gay Parade and Love Parades, the rise of street and neighbourhood parties, exotic festivals in the big cities and the 'leisure parks' along

arterial highways make it overwhelmingly clear that lack of vitality is certainly not a problem for the public space now (Burgers 1992; Oosterman 1993). On the contrary, in many cities the appeal to a large audience has gradually become a problem in itself. A large proportion of this vitality, however, is not a result of a cultural policy, but rather of economic regeneration . Its results are measured in numbers and spending power. The question of the cultural significance of this huge revival of urban enjoyment remains undiscussed or gets bogged down in the same old complaints about mass culture.

The Council of Europe documents are in any case remarkable in their explicit cultural-political objectives. These days we find no more than lip service being paid to the importance of 'meeting' in sundry policy documents. What this meeting consists of, or should consist of, why and when this is important, and what this requires of public space, remains entirely implicit.

Those who set the vitality of the city centres as a criterion for the success of the cultural ambitions of the urban planner can sit back contentedly. However, in the light of the new cultural geography, of which we have been sketching the outlines in the preceding paragraphs, a debate about the cultural implications of the new organization of space is needed – as it has perhaps been needed for the last 25 years.

The new spatial planning can be described as a collection of 'landscapes' that form the domain of various social sectors, interests or groups (cf. Zukin 1991). Dutch sociologist Jack Burgers distinguishes six landscapes of this kind: the erected public space (landscapes of fast-rising economic and governmental potential), the displayed space (landscapes of temptation and seduction), the exalted space (landscapes of excitement and ecstasy), the exposed space (landscapes of reflection and idolization), the coloured space (landscapes of immigrants and minorities) and the marginalized space of deviance and deprivation (1999). In combination these spaces form the postmodern city, but their toleration of one another is far from par for the course. 'The veneration attendant upon the exposed space can conflict with the ecstasy of the exalted space, for instance in the case of the invasion of a historically important city centre by hotels, restaurants and bars. The commerce of the displayed space can inflate prices in what was previously marginalized space' (Burgers 1999, p. 143). The various spaces are associated with differences in economic wherewithal and social influence. Some landscapes expand at the expense of others. It follows that a spatial planning policy that protects and sustains weaker landscapes is a necessity. The ambitions of cultural policy, however, should go beyond these social objectives, which can still be formulated in terms of equitability.

'If erected space towers above marginalized landscapes of unemployment and dependence on state benefits, if coloured space comes into being by means of coercive circumstances and not of freedom of choice, if exposed space serves only the cultural sophistication of the urban cultural elite, if the exalted space leads to street violence that makes people shut themselves up in their homes out of fear for their lives and property, if the displayed space becomes unaffordable for a growing proportion of the population, then the accessibility of the public space is threatened. In all these cases intervention is required' (Burgers 1999, p. 143).

This time the task for a new cultural-political intervention does not concern the vitality – that can safely be left to the commercial actors – but the creation of interfaces between the different 'landscapes'. It is in these interfaces that the new public domains can emerge.

An attentive observer will notice that the new planning briefs for public space all too often remain trapped within the various landscapes. Seldom does the design for the new public space focus on the interfaces or intersections of the various landscapes. Where is the confrontation between the economic landscape and the multicultural city formulated as a design brief? In what re-design of a railway station area is the confrontation between the station as a dynamic economic landscape and as a resting place for the marginalized addressed or included as part of the design? Brinckerhoff Jackson (1957) has shown that railway station environments are inherently a stacking of different spheres and diverse users. However, station design is mostly employed to actualize a spectrum of uses. The question is whether this is the only conceivable escape from the perceived problems of manageability. Would another programme of requirements not offer the designer the chance to better deal with that inherent layeredness of station environments?

In order to come to grips with the brief for the new public domain in which these various landscapes touch and overlap each other, we must gain insight into the cultural-political implications of the most important tendencies that currently structure these landscapes: parochialization, functionalization and aesthetization.

In the preceding paragraphs it emerged that the archipelago structure expresses itself in a parochialization of great tracts of public space. People increasingly use space à la carte, frequenting those exact events, festivals, schools and shops that conform to their identity and avoiding other places. This means that different groups in society follow different paths through space and time. The public space turns out, in reality, barely to function as a public domain; rather it is a transit zone between enclaves of different variations on 'our kind of people'.

Contemporary spatial segregation exists less and less in the fact that all the activities occur in a single location but rather in the fact that the spatial networks of certain groups barely overlap these days. Of course this also involves differences between groups. Some groups (senior citizens, poorly educated immigrants, children from less well-to-do backgrounds) are considerably less mobile than others. The name 'backseat generation' (Karsten 1993) is certainly not applicable to all young people; it refers specifically to children from middle-class environments. Similarly, many people know the Eurostar or Thalys high-speed trains at best as a train zooming by, while others use it to travel to and from EuroDisney for a long weekend away.

How should we interpret this reality of the public space as a collection of cultural-political parishes? Most evident is the discrepancy with the dominant cultural-political ideology of the public space as 'place of meeting'. In policy papers, the meeting function of the public space is a central objective. It is a romantic image, partly reinforced by historical-sociological studies in which it is suggested that this ideal existed in the past. The coffee houses of Vienna, the cafés and boulevards of Paris and the Palais Royal are the often-cited exemplars of real public space (Benjamin 1983; Sennett 1978; Berman 1982; Hetherington 1997), and always serve to support the notion that the public space is in decline.

Decline suggests that the public space used to serve as public domain, but fulfils this function less and less of late. This view is prominent in the essay collection Variations on a Theme Park, edited by Michael Sorkin (1992). The subtitle of this book is telling: The New American City and the End of Public Space. But just what kind of a public space was it that has come to its end? And is the notion of the 'end' of the public space in fact accurate? In order to answer these questions we must look in more detail at what the term parochialization actually means.

In addition to distinguishing between the public and the private sphere, the American sociologist Lofland distinguishes so-called parochial spaces (1998). Although open to the public, these are spaces that evidently constitute the space of a certain group: whoever wanders in as a stranger feels like a guest, often unwanted. The parochialization of public space, the appropriation by or for certain groups, is seen as one of the most important causes of the decline of the public space as meeting place (e.g. Gadet 1999). However, it is questionable whether the oft-cited real public spaces were not to a certain or even to a large extent parochial spaces, in an urban society that was also segregated then. Demarcations may not always have run along class or race lines, but it is certain that in the past, too, public and semi-public spaces derived their character from the groups that frequented these spaces.

This assessment leads to a surprising conclusion. Perhaps it is not parochialization that hinders the development of public domain, but in fact an overwrought idea of the public space as a neutral meeting place for all social groups regardless of class, ethnicity or lifestyle. The English sociologist Ray Pahl commented some time ago on what he sees as over-strained attention to the public life of the city: 'From this perspective of a particularly intense and complicated private life, one may wonder whether people have any need for this currently so touted vitality of the city.... I've heard those stories that emphasize that the pinnacle of urbanity is that one runs the chance of coming into contact with the unexpected. I think this is rubbish. It is a typical young man's concept of urbanity' (in Ooster-man and Van der Loo 1989). The last sentence implies: and thus a parochial view of urbanity.

In this case then, those who talk about the demise of the public space usually mean the demise of a certain kind of public space, which on closer examination often does display very parochial traits. Does this mean that public domain is defunct as an objective for a cultural policy? Is what remains merely a collection of parochial spaces? Or is it in this parochi-alization that we find the beginnings of public domain?

In the network society everyone puts their own city together. And so too does each citizen select his own public domain. This naturally touches on the essence of the concept of public domain. If the modern city can best be understood as a collection of landscapes, and if the citizen is constantly occupied in keeping his own small network intact with as little friction

with other groups as possible, then that does seem to mean the death of any form of public domain. But that is not how the individual space of the archipelago resident actually looks.

The paradox is that what many people experience as pleasant public space is in reality often dominated by a relatively homogeneous group. However, these are not the spaces dominated by one's own group. Anyone reflecting on personal 'public-domain experiences' will notice on closer inspection that the key experiences with shared use of space often involve entering the parochial domains of 'others'. Public domain is thus not so much a place as an experience. One experiences this space as public domain because one does not belong to that specific dominant group.

This paradox of the experiencing of public domain comes up again and again. John Urry (1990) remarked that tourists are put at ease by everyday things (eating, going shopping) in an exotic world. A public space is experienced as more pleasant the more the activities of the dominant group turn out to be variants on one's own everyday life, and thus foster participation rather than spectatorship.

Seen in this light, public domain is an experience at a location where the 'code of behaviour' is followed by groups with which we are not familiar. This entails an interesting paradox: the dominance of a certain group does not preclude the experience of public domain, but rather produces

On a summer's evening, the Gaasperplas Park in Amsterdam South-East is experienced as public domain because it clearly has its own atmosphere and one type of activity predominates: a variety of immigrants are picnicking. If a group of youths were to play football among these picnickers we would not be likely to experience this as public domain.

The daily market in The Hague does not present a cross-section of The Hague's populace, but someone who is unfamiliar with the market experiences it as public domain: it is rule-based behaviour dominated by another group.

The car beach at Rockanje has a distinctive Wild West atmosphere, but it is implicitly dominated by one certain group: the people driving their four-wheel drives. Spectators experience it as an exchange because they do not know that group (or its rules of behaviour), but they can legitimately walk around (in astonishment).

Tourists definitely experience Amsterdam's city centre as public domain because the city centre is not touristically overprogrammed. They are confronted with a cosmos of social behaviour whose rules they do not know. Precisely because the tourist does not yet threaten those rules, the presence of tourists is not experienced as problematic and the public-domain experience remains intact.

it. 'Citizens create meaningful public space by expressing their attitudes, asserting their claims and using it for their own purposes,' writes Peter Goheen (1998, p. 479). In this context Zukin (1995) talks about a 'symbolic economy', and there are strong and weak producers of meanings, commercial and avant-gardist, in this economy too, cultural products and cultural consumers, trendsetters and fashion victims. The point is: how open are those dominated domains, what relations do they have with others, and what can be designed from this.

This means that public spaces, just like enclaves, are in many cases defined by a form of 'parochialization'. Different groups seek to 'occupy' or at least dominate certain culturally significant public spaces (see Hayden 1996). This has both positive and negative effects. On the one hand the vitality and etiquette of a certain place guaranteed by the presence of an identifiable 'leading group' (Manuel de Solá-Morales refers to 'urban tribes'); on the other, parochial formation implies that certain groups or certain behaviour is excluded. This brings us back to a key theme of public domain. In the words of Zukin: 'The defining characteristics of urban public space [are] proximity, diversity, and accessibility' (quoted in Goheen 1998, p. 479). Successful public domain therefore requires a relatively strong group, without the position of that group leading to exclusion and repression. This does not rule out that the dominance over a certain space can be won by another group: public domain always presupposes the possibility of breaking through certain codes. When a space consists of multiple spheres, a group can dominate an important spot, while elsewhere the opportunities for other groups (or expressions) are safeguarded. Public domain as a sphere of exchange and confrontation in society presupposes the mutual proximity of different spheres much more than the fully shared use of one and the same space.

The core of successful public space thus lies not so much in the shared use of space with others, let alone in the 'meeting', but rather in the opportunities that urban proximity offers for a 'shift' of perspective: through the experience of otherness one's own casual view of reality gets some competition from other views and lifestyles. That shift of perspective, however, is not always a pleasant experience. Take the famous example of Baudelaire's The Melancholy of Paris (see Jukes 1990), which concerns the experiences of a young couple who are confronted with the staring eyes of street urchins while sitting in front of one of the gas-lit restaurants on the corner of one of the new Parisian boulevards. Their apparition in

the bright light shatters the self-determined mise en scène of romance and happiness and makes the presence of the man and his children a problem. The other Paris shows itself and the perspective shifts. It is a public-domain experience par excellence, but not a happy one.

Mixing functions and functionalization

There is a wonderful double map by Patrick Abercrombie on which he depicts his plan for London. The colours on the map show the mixture of work, home and traffic as it was in a pre-war London neighbourhood. In the second map, Abercrombie drafts the idealized vision of his plan for London. Abercrombie's separation of functions provided for the removal of business activity to special business sites on the edges of the neighbourhoods. There was always a transport route running between these business sites and the residential neighbourhood, so that the neighbourhoods would not only be relieved of industrial activity – polluting and noisy almost by definition – but also its attendant traffic. Until the 1960s, this principle of separation of functions was one of the ideals of the modern urban planner, and while the small-scale urban renewal of the 1970s and '80s arose partly as a critique of this, it stubbornly remained urban planning practise. It is to this planning and urban development that we owe the low-dynamism, monofunctional residential neighbourhoods and the 'business sites' on the outskirts of cities, as well as the 'recreation areas' with their characteristic standard picnic tables, cheap greenery and rough turf.

This doctrine of separation of functions is being jettisoned in a multitude of ways. Small-scale business activity is in many instances less polluting and less noisy and also proves to offer many advantages for the neighbourhood. The arguments in favour of a vital city are indeed often accompanied by a call for more space for small-scale business activity. Communal business buildings in the neighbourhoods, intensification of the programme of the postwar housing schemes: these are examples of the realization that the mixing of functions is in fact valuable in many cases. Indeed, it not only has value but also generates it. Old buildings converted for housing, recreation (in the form of theatre or fitness studios) and for business use turn out to be extremely profitable real estate – to the initial amazement of many project developers and investors. If old industrial buildings were still a hindrance ten years ago, these days they count as a blessing for the planning process, and are launched into the very heart of the design brief as 'industrial monuments'.

For the separation of functions based on ground use, also known as 'zoning', a different process comes into play. Behaviour is functionally programmed in a growing number of spaces. This cultural geography cannot be read from planning maps. It comes to the fore primarily in the way each space is now given a unique and exclusive sphere. These days, cultural policy is compiled from the cultural meanings of spaces, based on the way that places are connected with cultural identities, with life-styles, with certain social relationships. But we also take into consideration the way in which particular behaviours are forced or stimulated.

In our analysis, all kinds of spaces that could in principle be public domain are in essence functionally programmed. Indeed this analysis of a functionalization of the public space also throws a different light on Augé's analysis of these places as non-places. Augé does not recognize that these places are designed as non-places for functional reasons. The high priority given to 'crowd handling' in the design of many public spaces – from airport terminals to the foyer of a modern museum, from the station to the atrium of a department store – dictates a certain layout. Many non-places are not the result of a lack of design, but are in fact the explicit result of a proper execution of a plan brief! Augé also noted that the French national railway company, SCNF, suddenly starts to address travellers as 'passengers' once they board the high-speed TGV. That is merely a consequence of the functionalization of their behaviour. A similar process takes place at airports, albeit that here the transition from the zone of the 'shoppers' to the zone of the 'passengers' is continually being shifted further, in favour of retail space. Once one has entered the 'passenger' zone, the layout is dictated by the functional desire to lull passengers into a state of slumber, and if possible keep them that way. Flying itself is not without danger in any case, but the presence of large groups of people who must behave in a more or less disciplined manner in order to wait in an extremely restricted space, requires a functional programming of spaces. At the gate, after the security check, and most certainly in the aircraft, it is not the active, individual experience of the 'traveller' that is the main priority, but the efficacious 'conveyance of passengers' as a group. Breaking up the waiting process into a succession of short waits may be irritating to the traveller, but it is functional from

the viewpoint of 'crowd handling' and maintaining discipline. Once they have been induced into the slumber state, passengers are programmatically guided until they once again leave the terminal at their destination.

As a non-place, the airport is thus the explicit product of design. Augé's indignation implies that the non-place is the result of a lack of care, while here it is more a question of an excess of programming. The analysis of functionalization casts his romantic comparisons with the vitality of the 19th-century station in a different light.

Those who have a soft spot for the public domain must account for the fact that many places that bring together a great diversity of public are currently designed, very deliberately, as 'zero-friction' environments, as friction-free space. The design is dictated by the avoidance of friction. Airports are not the only place where public domain fails to come into existence because of an implicit cultural policy of functionalization. The dominant target image for new stations is as 'transfer machine', and the same is true for the shopping malls and the theme parks. Sadly we are also seeing this tendency in museums and in the cities. In museums, the 'piloting' of the streams of visitors is becoming an ever more important design task. It is not the optimum interaction with the art but the smooth outflow of the public that determines what is successful design.

The functionalization of city centres for the benefit of tourist consumption has not penetrated everywhere quite as far as in Salzburg. However, here too plans are being devised to stage city centres as friction-free spaces. One of the means to this end is the system of the 'speaking facade'. Tourists in the smaller cities in the western provinces of Holland (Haarlem, Leiden, Gouda, Delft) will have a chance to 'roam' with headphones with a radio link from one historical facade to another, pumping their ears with all kinds of information about the historic city. In essence, this not only shuts out the outside world but also implements a system that orchestrates the most ideal tourist corridors. In other words, functionalization is not just restricted to non-places; it is a more general trend.

The analysis of functionalization also throws a different light on the 'controversy' between Manuel de Solá-Morales and Michael Sorkin. De Solá-Morales argues that covered shopping centres are in fact the new public spaces of society, an assertion with which Sorkin disagrees entirely. De Solá-Morales is correct in stating that the rise of the shopping-mall phenomenon does not, in itself, necessarily spell the demise of the public space. But when he asserts that these new collective spaces can develop into public domain, provided they are designed well and are a good fit with the existing city, he glosses over the programmatic functionalization that malls imply. Sorkin, for his part, rather facilely ignores the fact that the level of social differentiation in shopping malls is often much higher than at any other spot in the urban field. In the 'food court', interaction between strangers does in fact take place. However, his criticism of the 'regulation' of the mall as collective space – 'There are no demonstrations in Disneyland' – is in general justified and ties in with the analysis of functionalization being suggested here. It is not only because of the limited accessibility, or the fact that it is only a 'collective' space rather than a 'public' one, that a shopping mall often does not function as public domain. Perhaps a bigger obstacle lies hidden in the fact that shopping malls are designed with one single and very specific objective in mind: shopping and spending. As this functionalization of the space is designed more effectively through design interventions, the more the mall loses its potential as a public domain. A very diverse public is represented in branches of Ikea, but the functionalization of the space implies a complete focus on the purchase and on consumption. The eateries before the cash registers do nothing to diminish this.

Theme parks, such as the Efteling, Six Flags, Disneyland or an aquarium, which all attract a public that is more diverse than in traditional urban spaces, are completely dominated by their functionalization. People stand packed together for long periods in a queue, yet this very rarely leads to confrontations. This is partly attributable to the sophisticated animation policy: the waiting masses are kept occupied. Nor is this programme in any way random. Globally speaking, the Disney Corporation probably has the most know-how about the creation and management of 'feel-good' environments: the animation of the public, the management of latent conflicts and the regulation of potentially deviant behaviour have been turned into a science. Periodically everyone performs one's part in this endlessly drawn out 'Truman Show', apparently having few problems with it.

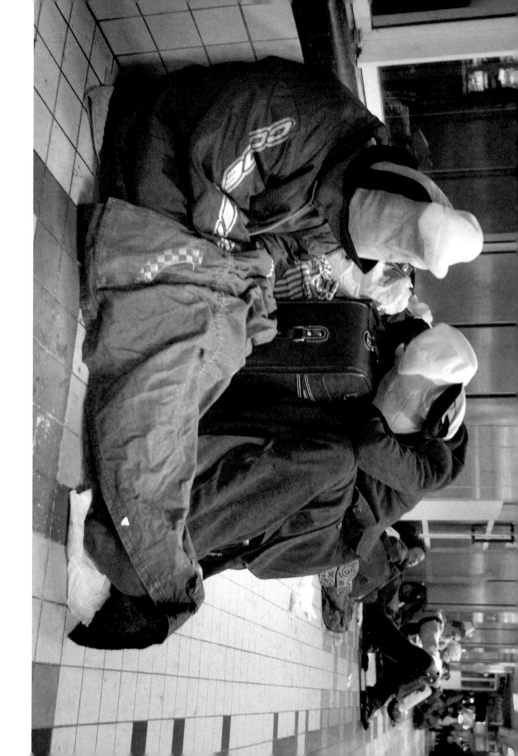

The upsurge of interest in the public space in the 1980s resulted in renewed attention to design. Design came to be seen as the solution for a multitude of issues, from the improvement of the image of the city to the complex problems in deprived metropolitan areas. Even though the urban culture figured high on the agenda of the revitalization policy for the cities, we have to note that design was inadequately embedded in the cultural-political strategy at that time. The new interest in the public space was superficial and naive in this regard. The city literally wanted to polish up its image with the rearrangement of the public space. The understanding of the public space as public domain remained confined to the notion that the public space would be more pleasant to spend time in if it were less disorderly. This was in part a reaction to the way in which public spaces had in years past been fragmented and filled in under pressure from all manner of interest groups. Resisting these claims became an important commitment, emptiness an aesthetic ideal. The layout of many public spaces thus became the object of 'design'.

Public spaces thus became part of a broad trend that has extended into all reaches of design. No functional object proves safe from 'design', from kitchen equipment by Alessi to designer jeans. A characteristic of this design trend is that any call for meaning seems to be dismissed. As Peter Jukes wrote as early as 1991: 'It seems ridiculous looking for deeper significance in designer phenomena: they are "fun", they "look good" – and that's all. Indeed, the term "designer" now extends over such a range of image-making, from graphics to film, that it seems to mean precisely the opposite of labelling: de-signed, the image is sundered from its significance: the aesthetic floats free, purged of any ethical content' (1991, p. 112).

What Jukes observes is in fact not a lack of signification, but the supremacy of a specific meaning. 'Fun' and 'looking good' are precisely the meanings that are expressed in the form and layout of many spaces, public or otherwise, such as cafés, museums and theatres. This involves turning to a formal idiom that is recognizable around the entire world. In the same way that the 'classical' design of the public space in the 19th century was associated with the rising urban class of the bourgeoisie, now the aesthetic ideal (perceived or otherwise) of this new urban middle class, the provision of services – the 'experts' or 'symbolic analysts' – dominates the new public space. 'Fun' is clearly something quite distinct from 'jolly'.

The observations of Jukes, viewed in this light, bring two themes to the fore that are important to our inquiry into the role of the design in the creation of public domain. In many cases design has the effect of what he calls 'de-sign', that is, the removal of the signs and meanings of a particular place. This dovetails into our cultural-geographical analysis, which shows that each place runs the risk of 'disappropriation', of the replacement of a multiplicity of meanings by that one which is given expression in architecture or layout and is redundantly confirmed by a signpost. What we are searching for is the room that the design can provide for the 'occupation' of the space with a multiplicity of meanings. Public domain, in this view, needs not 'de-sign' but rather 're-sign': the invitation to occupation by new meanings. And oddly enough Jukes' observation also provides a clue here: he implicitly points to the dominance of certain groups in the design of various public spaces. The production of the meaning of the public domain occurs in the field of tension between this dominance and exchange with other groups and activities.

101

The return of the 'politics of animation'

Twenty-five years ago, European governments in the Council of Europe developed an animation strategy for the cities. Within ten years this strategy was obsolete. This did not mean the end of the 'politics of animation', however. The cultural-geographical perspective shows that a new form of animation fuels not only the parochialization but also the functionalization of the public space. After all, the functionalization of places unfolds not just through the design, but also through the animation of the citizens in those spaces. The muzak of the shopping centres of the 1970s is a primitive example of animation. 'Feel-good' has since become a field with scientific underpinnings in which colour scheme, spatial arrangement, behaviour of shop personnel, the alternation of different kinds of goods, and the animation provided through a superimposed programme of fait divers are together meant to elicit an optimal frame of mind from the visitors.

The animation of the public space is back, but this time in a new form. While politicians are dreaming about socially positive meetings of different kinds of citizens, the public space has to a large extent been parochialized, and the places are being stage-managed through sophisticated

▷ Makassarplein (Makassar Square), Amsterdam

animation strategies. At airports one moves through feel-good zones into 'slumber areas', in shopping centres and malls the animation is directed at consumer behaviour. In theme and amusement parks a great diversity of people docilely share a limited space for hours without public domain even coming into play. The aestheticization is ultimately intended to animate but often precludes other alternatives.

Functionalization hinders the development of public domain. Perhaps this does not need to be said, but we are talking about functionalization rather than the separation of functions. The examples mentioned are increasingly characterized by a commingling of all sorts of functions and activities: the station as shopping centre, 'food court' and business meeting location. This distinction is important because the impact of animation coupled with functionalization can, of late, also be found in other domains. The town of Celebration is a manifestation of the application of these animation strategies to urbanization concepts. At the moment, city-centre animation is being examined in the Netherlands as a possible solution for 'mindless violence' in the evening. It might not be long before the expertise of the managers of the Efteling theme park is called upon to design the nightlife areas to this end, stage-managing them to curb aggression. This squares the circle. Twenty-five years ago, city councillors endeavoured to break through the dullness with animation, in consultation with sociologists; now they consult commercial experts in order to be able to control aggression. The layout and management of public spaces is dominated by an implicit cultural policy aimed at creating manageable, zero-friction environments. This is a strategy which is at odds with the development of public space into public domain being advocated here.

△ Bus station, Brasília

△ Little England zone in the Metro Centre shopping mall, Newcastle-upon-Tyne, England

In the preceding section the thinking about the public space was discussed in terms of the familiar typology and formal idiom. The design of public space according to the typology of the early-modern city does not suffice for the safeguarding and expansion of the public domain. Of course inspiration can still be drawn from classical references such as the city boulevard of Paris, the circuit of squares in Italian cities, and the 'squares' and 'crescents' of London, but the application of these typological references to the new places in the urban field does not automatically result in public domain. The same applies for the more detailed arrangement of the public space. The protective grate around the bases of trees that are once again popping up everywhere may well refer to these classical domains of urbanity, but this does not necessarily create the desired vitality, excitement or openness.

The use of the familiar typology and formal idiom illustrates the intention of government officials or commissioning entities to imbue the public space with new meaning. However, the actual creation of public domain demands a new approach to the relationship between form and meaning. In urban planning the relationship between the form of the public space and the use and socio-cultural meaning of these spaces was for a long time typological in nature. Squares not only had a form and layout that differed from streets or avenues, but there were associated differences in meaning and use that were understood by everyone. The same held for boulevards and parks, alleys and public gardens. This typology of public space made the city readable. For a number of reasons this relationship has been lost. One of these is that the clear typology of public spaces in modern urban planning has been watered down: streets and avenues became roads or child-friendly 'housing clusters' with speed restrictions, parks became 'park strips' or 'communal greenbelts', and

▷ Saturday evening, Leidseplein, Amsterdam

squares were assigned the function of 'sitting room' for the neighbour-hood or city. The public dimension vanished into a system of collective spaces; the urban space was transmuted into 'living environments'. The history of urban development today shows a series of initiatives meant to restore the lost relationship between form and meaning by turning back to the traditional urban planning typology of squares, parks, avenues, streets and public gardens.

The restoration of the urban planning features or characteristics of the 19th- and early 20th-century city is to this day being touted as the means to reverse the decline of the public in the urban space: from the plea of Jane Jacobs for the restoration of the block of buildings and the street with her 'side-walks', to the Planwerk Innenstadt Berlin, in which the ponderous task of saving the city and restoring the lost urban public dimension is translated in a classic 'Berliner' typology of blocks and enclosed spaces. In other cases this is done with a large dose of irony, as with the Citywalk at Universal Studios in Los Angeles, or with a longing – not quite devoid of commercial sense – for the traditional values of the 'small American town', as in the New Urbanism. This list could be extended with countless other examples, which all give evidence of an intensive hunt for the urban and the public, i.e. for public domain.

Merely imitating the formal characteristics of successful public spaces is, however, looking for the solution in the wrong place. The relationship between form and meaning is sooner watered down by the huge increase in mobility and the rise of a mass culture. The use of space 'à la carte' and the selective consumption of places, varied according to lifestyle, has fundamentally altered the meaning and the nature of the public space. Moreover, the insatiable appetite for new experiences among an ever-larger public leads to a totally different experience of places, whereby meanings are not predetermined whatsoever.

All in all, in current urban planning, form and meaning seem to have entered into an odd living-apart-together, off-and-on relationship. It is as if they drift in different worlds, and then here and there suddenly come together in an unexpected combination. This is brought to the fore most succinctly in the theme parks and shopping malls. New interpretations are based on forms that seem as if they were simply magicked out of thin air – as in The Mediterranean Village in the enormous Metro Centre mall in Newcastle-upon-Tyne. In other instances the little squares refer back to a lost imagined time – for example in the 'Little England' area, also in the

Metro Centre. The formal language of the classic public spaces of the early modern city is used in a slap-dash fashion in the large-scale shopping malls, such as West Edmonton Mall in Canada, the previously mentioned Metro Centre, or CentrO near Oberhausen. These are only some rather extreme examples of the way in which every space can, in principle, be 'themed'. This compulsion to add a theme has now started to have an impact on the 'real' city. The use of the classic typology and formal idioms in the quasi-public space of a mall does indeed instantly evoke the corresponding 'retro feel', but the replicas simultaneously affect the authenticity of the original: if you have encountered the 'artistic' portrait painters in the malls of Europe or North America you will look differently – and perhaps more realistically – at the original bohémiens in front of their little stalls on the quays along the Seine.

As we have shown, the lack of authenticity as such does not present an obstacle to the creation of public domain. If the development of public domain is served by a more 'urbanoid environment', a pseudo-urban environment such as the 'festival markets', which have also been called 'fruitopias', then the alleged lack of authenticity is of as little consequence as a discussion about something being beautiful or ugly, traditional or modern (see also Hannigan 1998). The commercial exploitation of the formal characteristics of historic public spaces (including the market square and the market hall), and the way this affects the historic city itself, very clearly demonstrate that the design of the public domain cannot be a question of simply mimicking these characteristics.

The essence of public domain, whether as regards a specific space like the Ramblas in Barcelona or a type such as the street, lies not in the formal characteristics but in the overlapping of and exchange between different social realms. The Ramblas is not simply a classic promenade with plane trees, but also a conjunction of 'chic and shabby', of mooching and busy road traffic, of history and modernity, a parade of foreigners and residents (Brinckerhoff Jackson 1957).

Yet even this orientation towards socially positive exchange and the shifting of perspective are not enough for our purposes. What's more, a too literal translation of this orientation toward exchange in fact undermines the concept of public domain. The notion of an 'absolute' and location-specific public domain that all the groups in society use must be jettisoned. This pure, politically-correct view of public domain as 'meeting',

as the Great Fraternization in the public space, forms the biggest hurdle for the creation of public domain.

In the network society everyone puts together their own city. Naturally this touches on the essence of the concept of public domain. The modern city is most easily understood as an archipelago of enclaves, and if the citizen is continuously occupied with maintaining his or her own small network with as little possible friction with other groups, then that does indeed ostensibly spell the demise of any form of public domain. However, that is not how the private space of the archipelago resident looks. The paradoxical fact is that many people are still searching for that experience of intensely felt public places. Public domain is, in our firm opinion, not so much a place as an experience.

Public domain experiences occur at the boundary between friction and freedom. On the one hand there is always the tension of a confrontation with the unfamiliar; on the other, the liberation of the experience of a different approach. In the main, our public domain experiences are in fact related to entering the parochial domains of 'others'. In these instances there is, on the one hand, the dominance of another group; on the other, there is the possibility of personally deciding how far one goes along with the experience.

Public domain centres around experiencing cultural mobility: for the opportunity to see things differently, the presentation of new perspectives, as much as the confrontation with one's own time-worn patterns. Being coerced to conform does not tally with this perspective of a properly func-tioning public domain. Being challenged to relate to others does.

The set of instruments

The view of public domain as a sought-after experience of other social worlds complicates the response to the question of public domain as a design exercise. The answer is not so much a case of the actual layout of separate spaces, but rather a conscious design of different spaces and their interrelationships. This does not mean that the design and layout of those separate spaces is unimportant. Safety and manageability play a leading role here. In this essay we have indicated that a dismissive attitude towards the increased demand for safety is misplaced. A sense of safety is often a precondition for full participation, so parties who want to facilitate exchange must bear this in mind. The trick is rather to prevent safety improvements being at the expense of the development of the public domain. In more general terms, it is a matter of thinking about the general urban planning conditions under which cultural and social exchange – the soul of an urban society – can flourish. Moreover, it is in fact also a question of physical conditions, of design and layout, and not simply of executing the urban programme as in many urban renewal strategies. The inadvertent effects of these programmatic strategies prove this. The attractiveness of certain urban spaces works to their disadvantage: they become over-populated and are often the arena for mindless violence. We must rekindle the lost relationship between the social and the physical space, between form and meaning, with an eye to differences and relationships, as well as bear in mind the demands of a mass culture in flux. The last section of this essay provides an impulse for this, exploring the possibilities of urban planning principles that have developed in the formation of that same mass culture.

We are referring to Sharon Zukin, who thinks that the trick is to 'frame encounters that are both intimate and intrusive'. Taking this further, we see three conceivable strategies for the design of public domain: theming, compressing and connecting. Theming and compressing focus on the creation of places that can become meaningful to specific groups. We have referred to these locations or spaces as 'spheres', which implies that means other than architecture can be employed to create them, for example from the world of theatre or the amusement park. Authenticity is then no longer a mark of quality. In the final analysis all authenticity is staged authenticity, and theming no longer disqualifies an object or space from being authentic. The key to compressing is the generation of public domain by bringing a number of elements that are meaningful for different groups into close proximity with one another. Not with '10-percent hindrance' as a goal, as in the years of architectural structuralism, but in order to generate public domain as experience.

In this context, connecting emphasizes the importance of the way in which different places are related to one another. Connecting can just as easily have a confrontational character as a seductive one, just as readily entail the direct opposition of two worlds as the suspicion of such a presence. (A comparison with the theatre, film and entertainment

industries crops up again here: montage, *mise en scène*, stage changes).
Not all confrontation is productive, and nor does all friction have a value
for a public domain. Design can contribute to a connection that makes
it possible to consider oneself conversant with the cultural dynamic in
different parishes or spheres. We will present a few examples.

Fences for public access

In the late 1980s a small battle broke out over Tompkins Square Park, a
small park square in New York's East Village. It had become a hangout
for the homeless, alcoholics and drug addicts. At a given moment, the
police attempted to bring the situation under control by closing the park
at night. The battle of Tompkins Square Park is a famous and almost
classic example of the battle for the meaning of public space (Smith 1992).
Was the police intervention really intended to fight displacement? Was it
really about the protection of public domain? Or did it in fact undermine
that very notion? Smith points to the fact that the attempt to tame the
culture of the park dovetailed perfectly with the strategy to improve the
neighbourhood by having new, erstwhile wealthier groups take the place
of the often-poor residents at the time, i.e. gentrification.

It is now possible to analyze the quality of Tompkins Square Park in
a different way. The park has been given a new lease of life. What is
immediately noticeable about the layout is the long stretches of fencing
that subdivide the park into different domains (as is the case with many
other squares in Manhattan). It seems like a relic from the days that the
police were trying to control the behaviour here. But in fact the multiple
fences fulfil another, independent function. Different groups have found
their own place in the small park: on a warm day the homeless occupy
the little benches along the pathways, the dog-owners can be found on the
enclosed sawdust plot, the youngsters play in the basketball cage, the
children play in their playground surrounded by heavy bars, and the
anarchists, the little families and the yuppies each sit on their own fenced-
in grass plots. Some critics regard the presence of these fences as proof
that Tompkins Square as an actual public domain has been abandoned
(Smith 1992). But isn't it much rather a case of the reverse? Tompkins
Square is an example of the value of compression and moderated parochialization. Various 'urban tribes' have appropriated places in the park,

and thereby display the population of the East Village in all its diversity in one small space. The fences are in essence symbolic orderings: they demarcate particular spheres, without harsh isolation or exclusion. Tompkins Square Park now is a stage on which everyone is simultaneously actor and spectator and is therefore an example of properly functioning public domain.

Fences have long been a feature of parks. Perhaps they form a somewhat too literal translation of the concept of 'framing', but in fact they are often only symbolic demarcations. Parks are the public gardens of the city, and by definition gardens are enclosed. Moreover, a fence marks a place. A fence around a public park shows that it is a special place where a particular use and behaviour is expected and where, in comparison with other public spaces in the city, precisely formulated rules apply.

This analysis of the value of demarcation for our approach to public domain casts a different light on a number of broadly accepted design principles. This symbolic significance of fences often sits uncomfortably with the principles of 'fluid space', openness, neutrality and collectivity found in modern urbanism. Replacing parks with communal green spaces is exemplary for the blurring of the concepts of public access and public domain in the work of the architects and urban planners of the modern school. Yet many of the contemporary plans for squares and parks are also designed as fluid spaces. The concept of 'fences for public accessibility' demonstrates an alternative design strategy for the development of public domain.

The well-designed compression and connection promote public access and exchange, but no one can expect a total solution from such design principles. Design strategies such as these also call for 'supportive policy': safety guarantees are fundamentally important.

Not far from Tompkins Square stands Stuyvesant Town. In its urban-planning typology it is the built reality of Le Corbusier's Plan Voisin (for an explicit comparison see Harvey 1989, p. 4). For many people it is thus the model for the way in which modernist urban planning has obliterated the small-scale diversity of the city. With Le Corbusier it was applied to Le Marais district in the heart of Paris; here it concerns a disruption of the structure of the East Village. At first glance, the massive residential complex looks like other homogenous, monofunctional complexes con-

▷ Syntagma Square metro station, Athens

Syntagma Square/Grande Bretagne/Panepistimiou
IMP CAESAR T AELIVS

structed in cities throughout North America and Europe after World War II, which are now known as multi-problem 'projects' – that is if they haven't been torn down or blown up. However, anyone who dares to enter the complex is surprised by a park-like, well-maintained and well-managed space: an oasis, which does indeed temporarily shut out the hectic rush of urban life. Stuyvesant Town shows that a collective, privately managed space can simultaneously be a public domain where others are not excluded, but are 'guests', i.e. subject to certain rules. And fences are the symbolic indications of the existence of those rules here as well.

The idea of 'fences for public access' brings to mind a more general question about the meaning of fences and new electronic security systems. Turnstiles at metro stations and electronic gateways at airports, in department stores, and now also in libraries and at schools are an unmistakable component of new public domains. Along with the ubiquitous closed-circuit video cameras they are the expression of a search for a technologically controlled environment. We are easily inclined to see these artefacts as restrictions on the public domain, but when do these barriers trouble anyone? The electronic gateways at airports in fact probably have a reassuring effect: the exclusion of deviant behaviour sustains our faith in safe air travel. The electronic gateway at the airport shows that the institutions we depend on are doing everything possible to guarantee our safety.

Important here is that the electronic screening with metal detectors at airports and in department stores and libraries is to a large extent objective. Exclusion is based not on appearance or attire, but on the presence of metal. What matters is the possession of (metal) objects that could pose a threat for the assembled public (airports), or of goods that have not been paid for (department stores) or not registered (libraries). The turnstile possesses a similar objectivity.

In these cases the technology is in fact an aid in the creation of public domain. In part these fences take the place of difficult individual, moral choices (Latour 1986): shall I pay for the metro or not, shall I steal that book or not. The electronic gateways do not only free us from such moral dilemmas, but can also make certain places more public: a library where you are only allowed entry with a pass or membership remains an exclusive facility and is not a public domain; a library that only checks whether a book has been signed out has the potential to develop into public domain.

124

The City Library in Rotterdam is an example of how a public library has developed into a public domain. This library is open to everyone, member or not. There are checks only at the exit using electronic gateways. The public makes massive use of the library and is diverse in composition. This diversity is also borne out by different atmospheres: the periodicals reading room, where dozens of people, mainly men of foreign origin, read newspapers from other countries; young people who surf the Internet; street people who sit playing chess at the chess tables located here and there; students who study in more remote corners; children (and adults) who sit reading comics; amateur historians who bury themselves in the history of the city, and the erudite scholars who consult the Erasmus Collection. And all this in a building whose huge space with escalators is reminiscent of a department store.

The safety discussion must not be sidestepped, but must be approached from the ideal of public domain. Some technologies can be of service to the concept of public domain, others much less so. The manifold use of video surveillance is much less objective than the detectors mentioned above, for instance. Closed-circuit TV is primarily used to 'preventively' keep an eye on 'suspect' groups. This often means that external features are taken as an important indicator of potential threats. In reality this can of course just as readily lead to deviant behaviour as discourage it: when 'marginal-group youngsters' have discovered the cat-and-mouse game they can play with the video-registration room, and then there is virtually no way to stop them playing that game!

Connecting the private and public worlds

The built collective spaces, such as malls and multiplex cinemas are becoming ever bigger and incorporate new functions every time. This means that they are becoming ever more complete worlds unto themselves; they have no relation with the outside world other than that they permanently suck in massive numbers of visitors and spew them out again. With respect to the Centre Pompidou, Baudrillard has defined this as 'implosion': the public space is sucked out until it becomes a vacuum, and then implodes. However, it is remarkable that in fact the opposite is true of the Centre Pompidou. The circulation around this building in fact fills the public space with activity: it generates a public for the spectacle that the building itself provides and it organizes a theatre on the forecourt by

▷ Lookout for plane-spotters close by Schiphol Airport, Amsterdam

attracting an audience and furnishing it with a mobile stage. The public looks down from the escalators at the theatre below; the people below look up at the movement in the Centre Pompidou. This quality of the public domain is decidedly not accredited its true worth, because as part of the recent renovation the escalators that were until recently freely accessible were closed to the non-paying public.

The Centre Pompidou illustrates how the private world of those ever-bigger collective crowd-pullers can be relevant to the public world of the city and the urban field. Just imagine if the dynamism of performances (moving parts of the Schouwburg theatre's scenery), and streams of public for the three big cultural venues (the Schouwburg, De Doelen concert hall and congress centre, and the multiplex cinema) – were visible from the newly designed Schouwburgplein in Rotterdam; the square would then be centre-stage for a marvellous and extremely diverse spectacle – and this without compromising the integrity of the spheres of theatre, music, and cinema.

'Liminal Spaces'

The new public domain does not only appear at the usual places in the city, but often develops in and around the in-between spaces in the archipelago of homogenous and specialized islands, in surroundings that belong to different social, economic and cultural landscapes. These places often have the character of 'liminal spaces': they are border crossings, places where the different worlds of the inhabitants of the urban field touch each other. A fairly broad group (Zukin, Shields, Sennett) supports the idea of the importance of 'liminality', though not everyone interprets it in the same way. Sennett (1990) puts the emphasis on the transitions between different spheres marked by 'weak borders', while Zukin (1991) settles for spaces that will surely be dominated by a specific forceful function, but simultaneously allow or even stimulate other interpretations and activities. The market place is the classical example of such a 'liminal space', more recent instances are mentioned above (see also the concept of 'framing' in Zukin 1995). However, these make it obvious how difficult it is to support 'liminal spaces'. An infamous example is the public space in the New York University Library on Washington Square. NYU was granted planning permission to build higher because the loss of light on the square would be compensated by a space open to the public in the beautiful library designed by Philip Johnson. Because of the weak boundaries between the serene atmosphere of the library and the relaxed atmosphere of the public space, the public accessibility was soon made subject to restrictions.

Another possibility is the organization of radically varied autonomous but accessible places that one might refer to as 'heterotopia', and thus 'organize a bit of the social world in a way different to that which surrounds them' (Hetherington 1997, viii). In this instance it is the contrast that is most important, the contrast with other places, the abrupt transition from one to the other. Public domain can even arise in an urban field that is composed of enclaves of various kinds, providing some dynamic is occasionally organized in that enclave landscape that breaks through the predictable (and often highly prized) peace of the enclaves. The perspective in heterotopias is shaken by interaction with other people or other cultural manifestations.

The above leads to the general conclusion that we must focus much more on the design of the transitions, the crossings, the connections and the in-between spaces than in the past. It is here that we can imagine public-domain experiences (confrontation with otherness, a change of perspective, an exchange). In fact this means a fairly fundamental change of perspective at every level of the organization of the urban field: infrastructure, logistics and traffic, the positioning of large-scale amenities, and so on. Urbanism's guiding principle was always division, after all. This led to the entanglement of different worlds: public and commercial spaces, pedestrian zones and car zones, public and private transport, outer and inner space, 'landscapes of power' and 'landscapes of marginality'. The critique of the dissection principle in modern urban planning has resulted in buildings such as De Meerpaal in the small Dutch town of Dronten, which is primarily characterized as hindrance, no matter how sympathetic it might be. 'Ten-percent hindrance' was the previously mentioned design principle of De Meerpaal's architect, Van Klingeren, but perhaps the public domain would have been served better by a little more respect for what people experience in their own parishes. The design task for the public domain does not rest on the intermingling, but in once again making sutures that connect those dissected worlds in the design of the in-between spaces.

A good example of a successful coupling of functional spaces to specific places is the exhibition space of Munich's museum for 20th-century art, the Lenbachhaus, in the Königsplatz metro station. A 100-metre-long gallery for temporary exhibitions was constructed between ground level and the platform. Travellers descending the escalator down into the metro have a wonderful view of the full length of the gallery.

In Santiago, Chile, a library has been established in a metro station in a similar fashion. It is the radical difference between the functionality of the public transport system and the specific meaning of the library or gallery as place that makes for an interesting, challenging coupling.

Another interesting example is the pseudo-library in a motorway restaurant near the Dutch-German border. The chesterfield armchairs, standard lamps, and traditional bookcases (with ladder), intimate the atmosphere of an 18th-century English country manor. It is a pastiche and aims to play on a superficial reference and sentiment. However, if you settle down in this odd sphere you will come to the conclusion that people on the fringes of the roadside restaurant have discovered this as a place they can call their own, which they actually use to read a book and engage in a little conversation with other marginalia, an alternative for the most obvious space to spend an evening, i.e. the living room at home.

More friction please

Many spaces do not develop because of the dominance of the sense of boredom and the lack of safety. Perhaps this also presents an opportunity for a new design strategy. The permanent shadow of tedium in transit spaces and the sense of a lack of safety in, for example, underground stations represent an opportunity to develop these monofunctional spaces into public domain. Amsterdam's Schiphol Airport promotes itself as an 'Airport City'. Schiphol PLC even publishes a brochure in which it presents its managers as the Mayor & Aldermen of Schiphol City Council. But behind this facade lies a shopping, leisure and travel corporation. Here especially, the idea of the shift in perspective can lead to other qualities. Metro stations can also be imagined differently.

Mobility and marginality

There are two important issues that demand the attention of designers and policy-makers as regards the inclusion of different worlds. First of all there is the re-thinking and re-design of the place of the car in the city and, in relation to this, the space for marginal groups in the public domain. Since the early 1980s, the revitalization of public space in the city has been practically synonymous with the exclusion of the car from that space: car-free pedestrian zones have become the norm, a norm that usually achieves the opposite of the intended result. Cheerless parking lots developed outside the car-free inner city or the shopping centre in the periphery; a desolation also descended on the car-free areas after shops closed. The growth of car ownership has now led to the evolution of a car world along the motorways: roadside restaurants have for a long time been more than just the place for a quick snack on the road, and are developing into places of entertainment and meetings; malls and leisure facilities are appearing at a number of locations in the urban field, which for all intents and purposes are only accessible by car.

These large-scale facilities are also typified by the same phenomenon: the car is left behind at the carpark or in the multistorey garage and people disappear into the car-free inner world. Isn't the division of functions repeating itself here? Is this the only strategy we can think up? Or is it more a question of the design of the liminal spaces here too?

Alex Wall has made a stirring appeal for a reintegration of the car in the public domain (1996). The dominant car culture is begging for a new

In his latest book, A Man in Full, Tom Wolfe gives an example of such a spectacle with his evocative description of 'Freaknic', when black students take to the streets of Atlanta once a year: 'Suddenly, as if they were pilots ejecting from fighter planes, black boys and girls began popping out into the dusk of an Atlanta Saturday night. They popped out of convertibles, muscle cars, Jeeps, Explorers, out of vans, out of evil looking little econo-sports coupes, out of pickup trucks, campers, hatchbacks, Nissan Maximas, Honda Accords, BMWs, and even ordinary American sedans' (p. 17). 'Oh, these black boys and girls came to Atlanta from colleges all over the place for Freaknic every April, at spring break, thousands of them, and here they were on Piedmont Avenue, in the heart of the northern third of Atlanta, the white third, flooding the streets, the parks, the malls, taking over Midtown and Downtown and the commercial strips of Buckhead, tying up traffic, even on highways 75 and 85, baying at the moon, which turns chocolate during Freaknic, freaking out White Atlanta, scaring them indoors, where they cower for three days, giving them a snootfull of the future' (p. 19). These black students are actually doing nothing different to what white students have always done, with an important difference: instead of descending on beaches and in the coves of seaside resorts, they descend on the streets of downtown Atlanta.

The development of the motorway as urban highway, as for example in Barcelona, offers it the potential of becoming a new type of boulevard, with the possibility of overlaps or interchanges with other transport systems and facilities at a number of places.

Parks on the edge of the city with lots of sports activities, where cars are parked in a parking area, can grow into 'sports worlds' by integrating them with other transport systems. The extension of the centre of the new Dutch town of Almere is constructed from different layers that are divided (and connected) by an arched ground level, below which the car dictates the scale, and a Camillo Sitte-like world for the pedestrian above it. The way that the facilities 'pierce through' the layers continually interpolates these two worlds.

kind of public space, where the car becomes part of the urban spectacle of looking and being looked at: 'promener en auto'.

The task lies in the reintegration, or at least realignment, of different mobilities. The car must also once again be included in the design of the public domain, certainly now that we realize that this is spread across the car-dominated urban field.

Space for marginality

The litmus test for the public character of a space is undoubtedly whether the homeless, or 'street people', are excluded or not. The issue is broached rhetorically in Susan Fainstein's statement that creating entertainment spaces where people enjoy themselves, even if that makes some people feel like outcasts, is not in itself so terrible (1994). This naturally leads to another – genuine – and much more interesting question, namely what makes people feel like outcasts and why certain people are in fact excluded. Sellers of the magazine for the homeless are barred from trains and the metro. Why? Because they make the passengers feel unsafe, say the directors of the U-Bahn in Berlin, for example. However, one of the reasons that the magazine was established was to afford the homeless a legitimacy for their request for a contribution to their subsistence. The homeless, street performers, pedlars and other 'street people' are not only excluded from shopping centres, malls, metro stations and other privatized spaces, but are also rarely welcome in the public domain. Whole factories run on the manufacture of benches that have been designed so that you cannot lie down on them. Rationally, it seems as if the efforts of revitalization strategies are exclusively aimed at reducing of the number of street traders, buskers and prostitutes in the environs of a square or park.

Public domain supposes that there is also space for these groups. Here too lies a design brief. In our opinion, the strategy of the homeless magazines, aimed at legitimizing the homeless in the streetscape, could be afforded a spatial pendant.

The assignment

In the introduction we mentioned a number of key tasks for the design of the public space over the coming years. Firstly, the development of the areas around the new HST stations, then the strategy for the inner cities – addressing the tension between the value as an attraction and attractiveness in particular – and thirdly the disquiet about violence on the street.

The artwork looks like a cross between a bench and a central-heating radiator. And on closer inspection that turns out to be exactly what it is: it is a bench linked to the district heating's network of pipes under the pavement. The artwork provides a comfortable seat or sleeping place and does not simply legitimize the presence of the homeless on the street, but is also an invitation to them to lie down and rest. It would be possible to create similarly comfortable spots for street traders, sheltered from the elements, weather and wind, and ditto pick-up places for street prostitutes, instead of their being banished to an industrial area. Daytime meeting places for drug addicts break the tragic ritual of junkies being moved on in order to keep the public space 'free' for the purpose of revitalization. Here design could contribute to the alleviation of the nuisance. A 'balise urbaine', or 'urban lifebuoy', is a combination of a piece of furniture and a building that is meant to answer the needs of the homeless. The plan was presented in Paris by Emmanuelle Lott and Jean-Marc Giraldi in association with the architect Chikpéric de Boisuillé and the philosopher Paul Virilio. The plan concerned small buildings of 100 to 150 square metres that provide reception space, lockers, telephone, postboxes, showers and washing machines, as well as information about work (namely temporary jobs in the neighbourhood). This intervention is controversial. Isn't design being used to mop up the mess? Isn't it merely helping people to survive, rather than offering real places to live? Of course design does not solve the problem of the homeless, but it could indeed be applied to alter the attitude to the question of the public space using symbolic beacons. The 'balises urbaines' are possibly the next step after the homeless magazines. The effect of the homeless magazines and their sale is of course not limited to the fact that the homeless legitimately supplement their income; it alters the relations in the public space because transactions now actually take place between marginal street-sellers and the public, and it hauls the homeless out of the sphere of a hopeless existence. A next step could be further integration by allowing them to sell cultural periodicals: a new version of Time Out, an improved Village Voice, or a new concept for the Uitkrant listings weekly, or even national news magazines. Henceforth, the elite would learn about what is going on culturally from the homeless.

Another example of the way in which design can be applied to marginality is the 'homeless vehicle' by Wodiczko. This New York-based designer developed a hood and extension system for shopping trolleys, offering the homeless not just a dry place to sleep, but also an enclosed space to carry their few precious belongings. However, the most important quality of the 'homeless vehicle' was its form: the hood gave the shopping trolley the shape of a space capsule, symbolically turning the powerlessness of the homeless in the streetscape on its head. The design never went into production.

Conversely, SRO's, cheap hotels where people rent a room for a month, a year or longer, can offer facilities that are also interesting for groups other than roomers or boarding-house residents. In San Diego there are three, designed by Quickley.

As a last more fundamental task we asked what we are doing with the new 'collective' but not necessarily public spaces in the urban field, at airports, amusement parks, factory outlets, etcetera.

The text has made it clear that the design of these places is to a large extent determined by the notion that frictionless public space is good public space: zero-friction architecture is the norm for HST stations; in the face of declining employment inner cities see no alternative to stream-lined tourist consumption; the battle against street violence is fought with more lighting, more surveillance cameras, a clearer organization and a great deal of appeal to one's moral senses: e.g. 'This is a violence-free zone.' Finally, in the urban field, we have thus far left the design of the public space entirely in the hands of other parties. In this essay we have demonstrated how this leads to the functionalization of the space, which in many cases cripples the creation of public domain. Versus this functionalization we see the imitation of the formal characteristics of classic public spaces, but this is only a pathetic gesture that achieves the opposite of what is actually intended.

Paradoxically, the emptying of the public space fills it with a single dominant meaning. We have shown that a concept of a 'pure' public domain is possibly a considerable stumbling block for creating that very domain. In contrast with this, we understand the public domain as an experience of other worlds. We often encounter public domain at places that are dominated by particular groups; that is precisely where the quality of the experience originates. Public domain then supposes that the exchange and commingling of those different worlds and their liminal spaces will become the design task. It also assumes the existence of places where this is possible: despite the diversity of the public, the high streets may be key shopping areas but are almost meaningless as public domain. We have shown that the coupling of relative freedom and technical provocation does indeed imbue the Schouwburgplein in Rotterdam with these qualities. That is the crux of the design task. That is the reason we have mentioned not only all the threats (tenaciously persistent parochialization, functionalization and aestheticization), but also a number of instruments: a thematic approach in a new sense, framing, compressing, coupling and connecting. Taking this further, fences and metal detectors can be given a completely different meaning. Lastly, we have given a number of impulses that demonstrate how the impact of those instruments becomes tangible. This is expressly intended as a challenge to architects, urban planners, policy-makers and cultural entrepreneurs.

Literature

Augé, M. (1992)
Non-Places. Introduction to an
Anthropology of Supermodernity
trans. J. Hope (1995) London: Verso

Baudrillard, J. (1977)
L' effet Beaubourg, implosion et dissuasion
Paris: Edition Galilée

Bauman, Z. (1995)
Life in Fragments. Essays in Postmodern
Morality Oxford: Blackwell

Beck, U. (1986)
Risikogesellschaft – Auf dem Weg in eine
andere Moderne Frankfurt/M.: Suhrkamp

Beck, U. (1993)
Die Erfindung des Politischen Frankfurt/M.:
Suhrkamp

Bell, D. (1978)
The Cultural Contradictions of Capitalism
New York: Basic Books

Benjamin, W. (1983)
Das Passagen-Werk Frankfurt /M: Suhrkamp

Berman, M. (1982)
All that is solid melts into air: the experiece
of modernity New York: Simon & Schuster

Bianchini, F. and Schwengel, H. (1991)
'Re-imagining the City' in: J. Corner and S.
Harvey, eds. (1991) Enterprise and heritage
London: Routledge, pp. 212-263

Brinckerhoff Jackson, J. (1957)
'The Strangers Path' in: Landscape 7 (1957)
1; reprinted in: J. Brinckerhoff Jackson (1977)
Landscapes in Sight. Looking at America
New Haven: Yale University Press, pp. 19-29.

Burgers, J., ed. (1992)
De uitstad: over stedelijk vermaak Utrecht: Van
Arkel

Burgers, J. (2000)
'Urban landscapes: On public space in the
post-industrial city' in: Journal of Housing
and the Built Environment, Vol. 15-2
pp.145-164

Casey, E.S. (1997)
The Fate of Place. A Philosophical History
Berkeley: University of California Press

Castells, M. (1996)
The Information Age: Economy, Society and
Culture – Vol. 1: The Rise of the Network
Society Malden, Mass./Oxford: Blackwell

Crawford, M. (1988)
Ecology of Fantasy Los Angeles: The Los
Angeles Forum for Architecture and Urban Design

Davis, M. (1998)
Ecology of Fear. Los Angeles and the
Imagination of Disaster New York: Metropolitan
Books

Fainstein, S. (1994)
The City Builders: Property, Politics and
Planning in London and New York Oxford:
Blackwell

Gadet, J. (1999)
Publieke ruimte, parochiale plekken
Ph.D. dissertation, University of Amsterdam

Gareau, J. (1991)
Edge City: life on the new frontier New York:
Doubleday

Giddens, A. (1994)
'Living in a post-traditional society' in:
U. Beck, A. Giddens, S. Lash, eds. Reflexive
Modernization. Politics, tradition and
aesthetics in the modern social order
Cambridge: Polity Press

Goheen, P. (1998)
'Public Space and the Geography of the
Modern City' in: Progress in Human
Geography 4 (22),
479-496.

Hajer, M. (1994)
De stad als publiek domein Amsterdam: WBS

Hajer, M. (1995)
The Politics of Environmental Discourse
Oxford: Oxford University Press

Hajer, M. and Halsema, F. (1997)
Land in Zicht! Een cultuurpolitieke visie op
de ruimtelijke inrichting Amsterdam: Bert
Bakker

Hannigan, J. (1998)
Fantasy City. Pleasure and profit in the
postmodern metropolis London/New York:
Routledge

Harvey, D. (1989)
The Condition of Postmodernity Oxford: Basil
Blackwell

Hayden, D. (1995)
The Power of Place – Urban Landscapes as
Public History Cambridge, Mass.: MIT Press

Hetherington, K. (1997)
The Badlands of Modernity – Heterotopia
& Social Ordering London: Routledge

Hitzler, R. (1988)
Sinnwelten Opladen: Westdeutscher Verlag

Hitzler, R. and Honer, A. (1994)
'Bastelexistenz. Über subjektive
Konsequenzen der Individualisierung' in:
U. Beck and E. Beck-Gernsheim eds. (1994)
Riskante freiheiten Frankfurt/M.: Suhrkamp,
pp. 307-315

Ibelings, H. (1998)
Supermodernism. Architecture in the Age of
Globalization Rotterdam: NAi Publishers

Jacobs, J. (1961)
The Death and Life of Great American Cities
New York: Vintage

Jameson, F. (1991)
Postmodernism or the cultural logic of late
capitalism London: Verso

Jukes, P. (1990)
A Shout in the Street. An Excursion into the
Modern City London: Faber & Faber

Karsten, L. (1995)
'Het kind in de stad: van achterbank-
generatie en "pleiners"' in: Geografie 4 (5)
36-40

Keith, M. and Pile S., eds. (1993)
Place and the Politics of Identity London:
Routledge

Latour, B. (1986)
'Technology is society made durable' in: J.
Law, ed. (1991) A Sociology of Monsters:
Essays on Power, Technology and
Domination London: Routledge

Lehnert, G. (1999)
Mit dem Handy in der Peepshow. Die
Inszenierung des Privaten im öffentichen
Raum Berlin: Aufbau-Verlag

Lefebvre, H. (1974)
The Production of Space trans. D.
Nicholson-Smith (1991) Oxford: Blackwell

Lofland, L. (1998)
The Public Realm. Exploring the city's
quintessential social territory
New York: De Gruyter

Mennell, S. (1976)
Cultural Policy in Towns Strasbourg: Council of
Europe

Merrifield, A. (1996)
'Public City : integration and exclusion in urban life' in: CITY 5/6 57-72

Netherlands, the. Ministry of Culture (1979)
De recreatieve stad Den Haag: SDU

Newman, O. (1972)
Defensible Space: people and design in the violent city New York: Macmillan

Oosterman, J. (1993)
Parade der Passanten. De stad, het vertier en de terrassen Utrecht: Jan van Arkel

Oosterman, J. and Loo, H. van der (1989)
'Achter de hele façade van de huidige stedelijke glitter gaat een harde realiteit schuil. In gesprek met Herbert Gans en Ray Pahl' in: Plan 3/4, 28-30

Pine, B. and Gilmore, J. (1999)
The Experience Economy: Work is Theatre & Every Business a Stage Boston: Harvard Business School Press

Prigge W. (1998)
'Vier Fragen zum Auflösung der Städte' in: W. Prigge, ed. Peripherie ist überall Frankfurt/ New York: Campus

Reijndorp, A. et al. (1998)
Buitenwijk. Stedelijkheid op afstand Rotterdam: NAi Publishers

Reijndorp, A. (1995)
'The Architecture of More Ecologies. Schijn en werkelijkheid van L.A.' in: Expeditie L.A. Rotterdam: NAi Publishers

Sennett, R. (1978)
The Fall of Public Man. On the social psychology of capitalism New York: Vintage

Sennett, R. (1990)
The Conscience of the Eye. The Design and Social Life of Cities New York: Alfred Knopf

Shields, R. (1991)
Places on the Margin London: Routledge

Simpson, J.A. (1976)
Towards cultural democracy Strasbourg: Council of Europe

Smith, N. (1992)
'New City, New Frontier: The Lower East Side as Wild, Wild West' in: M. Sorkin, ed. (1992) Variations on a Theme Park. The New American City and the End of Public Space New York: Hill & Wang, pp. 61-93

Solá-Morales, M. de (1992)
'Openbare en collectieve ruimte. De verstedelijking van het prive-domein als nieuwe uitdaging' in: OASE no. 33, 3-8

Sorkin, M., ed. (1992)
Variations on a Theme Park. The New American City and the End of Public Space New York: Hill & Wang

Sudjic, D. (1992)
The 100 Mile City London: André Deutsch

Urry, J. (1990)
The Tourist Gaze. Leisure and travel in contemporary societies London: Sage

Urry, J. (1995)
Consuming Places London: Routledge

Wall, A. (1997)
'Stroom en Uitwisseling – Mobiliteit als een kwaliteit van stedelijkheid' in: B. Colenbrander, ed. Mutaties Rotterdam: NAi Publishers, pp. 24-41

Zukin, S. (1991)
Landscapes of Power. From Detroit to Disney World Berkeley: University of California Press

Zukin, S. (1995)
The Cultures of Cities Cambridge, Mass.: Blackwell

Maarten Hajer (b. 1962)
holds the Chair in Public Policy at the Department of Political Science at the Amsterdam School for Social Science Research (ASSR) and the Amsterdam Study Centre for the Metropolitan Environment (AME), both departments within the University of Amsterdam. His publications include De stad als publiek domein ('The City as Public Domain') initially published in 1989, and followed by a revised and expanded edition in 1994; Land in zicht! Een cultuurpolitieke visie op de ruimtelijke inrichting ('Land ahoy! A cultural-political vision for spatial organization'), edited with Femke Halsema (1997), and The Politics of Environmental Discourse (Oxford, 1995).

Arnold Reijndorp (b. 1948)
studied Architecture at the Delft University of Technology. He then worked for the City Planning department in Rotterdam and was a lecturer in Urban Sociology at the University of Amsterdam. More recently he has been working as an independent researcher and commentator on the cutting-edge of architecture, urbanism and cultural developments in the urban environment. He has published several books and a series of articles about topics such as lifestyle and housing, the new suburbs, renewal in deprived neighbourhoods, and public space. He has been a guest lecturer at various universities and schools of architecture in the Netherlands and abroad. From October 1998 to October 2000 he was visiting professor in Urbanism and Urban Sociology at the University of Technology, Berlin.

Photographs

This research and publication of the findings was in part supported by a subsidy from the Netherlands Architecture Fund. The authors would especially like to express their thanks to: Francine Houben, one of the initiators of this project; Ivan Nio, who played an important role in the development of this publication; Bert van Meggelen for chairing the two discussion meetings, and Kitty Molenaar for the concept and design of the photographic essay.

Authors **Maarten Hajer** and **Arnold Reijndorp**
Translator **Andrew May**, Amsterdam
Editor **Els Brinkman**, Amsterdam
Photo Editors **Kitty Molenaar** and **Véronique Patteeuw**
Design **Kitty Molenaar**, Amsterdam
Lithography and printing **Die Keure**, Bruges, Belgium
Production **Véronique Patteeuw**
Publisher **Simon Franke**

An earlier version of this text was presented during discussion-meetings, held on January 27 and March 23, 2000.

Thanks to **Fons Verheijen**, Verheijen, Verkoren & De Haan Architects Bureau, Leiden | **René Boomkens**, Groningen | **Lia Karsten**, Bureau Karsten, Amsterdam | **Ruud Ridderhof**, Urban Development Service, The Hague | **Maaike van Stiphout**, DS landscape architects, Amsterdam | Dirk van Peijpe, Department of Urban Planning and Pubic Housing, Rotterdam | **Michael van Gessel**, Amsterdam | **Huub Juurlink** and **Cor Geluk**, Juurlink & Geluk, Rotterdam | **Hans Krop**, Heeling, Krop, Bekkering, Groningen/The Hague | **Hans Mommaas**, University of Brabant, Tilburg | **Ashok Bhalotra**, Kuiper Compagnons, Rotterdam | **Joke Klumper**, Mecanoo, Delft | **Tracy Metz**, Amsterdam | **Simon Franke** and **Barbera van Kooij**, NAi Publishers, Rotterdam | **Floris Alkemade**, Office for Metropolitan Architecture, Rotterdam | **Matthijs Bouw**, One Architecture, Amsterdam | **Paul Achterberg**, Quadrat, Rotterdam | **Ruud Brouwers**, the Netherlands Architecture Fund, Rotterdam - **Roemer van Toorn**, Amsterdam | **Edzo Bindels**, West 8, Rotterdam | **Joke van der Zwaard**, Rotterdam.

Available in North, South and Central America through D.A.P./Distributed Art Publishers Inc., 155 Sixth Avenue 2nd Floor, New York, NY10013-1507, Tel. +1 212 6271999, Fax +1 212 6279484. Available in the United Kingdom and Ireland through Art Data, 12 Bell Industrial Estate, 50 Cunnington Street, London W4 5HB, Tel. +44 (0)208 7471061, Fax +44 (0)208 7422319.

Printed and bound in Belgium

ISBN 90-5662-201-3